The 8 Financial Breakthroughs

The Ultimate Guide to Building Wealth for Your Financial Future

BY

Alvin Darien II

&

The Financial Pro Network Innovation Team

THE 8 FINANCIAL BREAKTHROUGHS

Copyright © 2024 by Alvin Darien II and Financial Pro Network.

All rights reserved. No part of this publication may be reproduced, distributed, or transmitted in any form or by any means, including photocopying, recording, or other electronic or mechanical methods, without the prior written permission of the author, except in the case of brief quotations embodied in critical reviews and certain other non-commercial uses permitted by copyright law.

Ordering Information: Quantity sales. Exclusive discounts are available on quantity purchases by corporations, associations, and others. Orders by U.S. trade bookstores and wholesalers.

For more information, books, corporate discount plans, media, and speaking engagements.
Email: info@fpneducator.com

www.DreamStartersPublishing.com

FPN INNOVATION TEAM

Disclaimer

All rights reserved. No part of this book may be reproduced in any form without the prior permission of the author and the publisher, except for training purposes.

No statement in this booklet is intended to form a contractual agreement or to modify or supplement any existing contractual agreement with any company, the author, the publisher, and members.

The author, the publisher, or any other entity shall have neither liability nor responsibility to any person or entity with respect to any loss or damaged caused, or alleged to have been caused, directly or indirectly, by the information contained in this book.

This book is sold with the understanding that the publisher and author are not engaged in rendering legal, accounting, or other professional advice or services. The views and opinions expressed in this book are the views of Alvin Darien II and do not necessarily reflect the views and opinions of any person or company.

Every individual's financial DNA is different, and the information contained herein may not be suitable for your current situation. You should seek the services and products of a competent professional before starting any financial program.

Table of Contents

Testimonials 5

Thank You 9

Introduction.. 11

Building Financial Awareness (*Breakthrough #1*)............... 16

Protection (*Breakthrough #2*) 27

Considering Your Cash Flow Needs (*Breakthrough #3*) 37

Debt-to-Income Ratio (*Breakthrough #4*) 47

Liquidity (*Breakthrough #5*) 59

Liquidity and Opportunity... 70

Shaping Your Future Income (*Breakthrough #6*)................. 82

Building Your Net Worth.. 94

Improving Your Conversations About Net Worth 105

Your Legacy (*Breakthrough #7*) 114

Establishing Your Business Legacy 121

Accountability (*Breakthrough #8*) 136

The Four Levels of Wealth 149

The Legacy Ladder 162

Conclusion 170

Testimonials

"**The 8 Financial Breakthroughs** is a state-of-the-art client analysis tool. It provides an extremely thorough analysis of the client's financial situation. This thorough analysis allows for highly effective and more importantly specifically designed solutions for the client. It is also an analysis tool that is effective and useful in the hands of any financial professional regardless of their experience and knowledge."
Ken Brownlee - Financial Industry Leader & Mentor

"Using **The 8 Financial Breakthroughs** with my clients helps them capture a complete understanding and vision of where they are and where they want to be. Helping them to build up their financial awareness and giving them the confidence to protect themselves from all the threats that exist around their money and legacy, empowers them to make better decisions. **The 8 Financial Breakthroughs** not only give you the blueprint to build your financial house, but it also prepares you for making upgrades along the way to help you increase your money and legacy's value for your family. Finally, we have a book that's a game changer to help you go from financial education to implementation, which holds you accountable for transforming a financial goal and dream into a reality!"

THE 8 FINANCIAL BREAKTHROUGHS

Andre Parker - Financial Industry Leader

"**The 8 Financial Breakthroughs** work like a financial GPS that will take you from where you are to where you want to be financially. They are a road map to creating generational wealth. Once a person or family starts on this path, they will wipe out poverty in their family in less than one generation. We will help millions of families using The 8 Financial Breakthroughs."

Earl McMillan - Managing Partner of Business Legacy Capital

"Financial Illiteracy is the pandemic issue that must be resolved. 5 Billion people worldwide and 75%+ of American adults have flunked a basic financial literacy quiz. **The 8 Financial Breakthroughs** is the answer to the financial literacy issue and provides the practical solutions that can be implemented to change your family's financial legacy!"

Gus and Renee Tucker - Financial Industry Leaders & Acquisition Manager

"**The 8 Financial Breakthroughs** will transform your life and aid in unlocking new levels of financial freedom and security while enjoying lasting success."

Curtis J. Williams - Financial Industry Marketing Innovator

FPN INNOVATION TEAM

"Employing **The 8 Financial Breakthroughs** is crucial to a client's ability to get a grip on their financial future. It is imperative that clients are financially aware of the threats that can derail their financial legacy. So as a financial educator it is important that we impress upon our clients the importance of maintaining a healthy debt to income ratio as well as liquidity in the form of an emergency fund. All of this can be achieved by selecting a competent financial professional to ensure that the client remains on track."

Robert and Adrian Johnson - Financial Industry Leaders

"**The 8 Financial Breakthroughs** has been a milestone in my career. It has positioned me to listen, be more relatable, and to customize a suitable plan that caters to my client's Financial DNA. My financial awareness helps me create more future income for my clients as well as creating generational wealth through legacy and succession planning. The 8 Financial Breakthroughs has been a major accountability source for my clients and for me."

Jameson Jenkins – Financial Agribusiness Consultant

THE 8 FINANCIAL BREAKTHROUGHS

"As I delved into **The 8 Financial Breakthroughs**, I noticed multiple things in my life became better. It all stemmed from an invaluable foundation created by arguably the most important breakthrough, accountability. The only time knowledge becomes power is when it is applied. Let's all seize control of our financial destined and pave the way for abundance in our lives and beyond."
Kaden Perron - FinTech Innovator

"I applied **The 8 Financial Breakthroughs** to change my financial habits. I worked on my custom blueprint to become debt free and changed my bad spending habits. Today, I am debt free, saving more money, back on track for building wealth for retirement and leaving a legacy."
Emma Colton - Financial Industry Leader

"I am more than appreciative of **The 8 Financial Breakthroughs** concept. It has helped guide my family's money plan with new clarity. Having a step-by-step guide to point us in the right direction has been a blessing. It gave us the chance to correct the mistakes we made, and we are grateful. We are on our way to doing much better and remaining that way... Shoutout to the FPN family for bringing this to the table."
Eddie & Tia Crockett - Financial and Business Coaches

FPN INNOVATION TEAM

Thank You

To our incredible Financial Pro Network (FPN) Innovation Team, words cannot express my deepest gratitude for your invaluable contribution to **"The 8 Financial Breakthroughs."**

Your tireless dedication, countless hours of hard work, and unwavering commitment to excellence have transformed this book into a beacon of financial wisdom. Your innovative ideas and keen insights have enriched every page, making it a truly empowering resource for readers. Thank you for your passion, your expertise, and your unwavering support throughout this journey.

Because of your extraordinary efforts, **"The 8 Financial Breakthroughs"** will undoubtedly educate and transform countless lives. You are the heart and soul of this project, and I am forever grateful for your remarkable contributions.

THE 8 FINANCIAL BREAKTHROUGHS

"Make sure you have financial intelligence…I don't care if you have money or you don't have money…you need to go and study finance no matter what."

Daymond John

FPN INNOVATION TEAM

Introduction

Whether you are considering making financial changes, managing debts and liabilities, or planning for retirement and your legacy, the first step is learning about finance and building your financial awareness.

As a financial professional, one of the most essential parts of my role is educating—teaching you how to keep moving toward your financial goals rather than distancing yourself from them.

It does not matter where you are or who you are; everybody needs to learn about personal financial basics. After all, just about everything around us is affected by financial literacy.

Once you have been educated about financial basics, it is all about acting on your decisions. But to make those decisions, you must first learn and establish positive financial habits. Then, you can take the necessary steps to improve and implement your financial goals.

Where Are You on Your Financial Timeline?

While we're all on a financial journey, everyone's financial timeline differs.

THE 8 FINANCIAL BREAKTHROUGHS

Perhaps you just purchased a home, moved to a new city or state, experienced a divorce, got married, or started a family. Maybe you are approaching retirement or have just retired. You need to make the right financial choices during any of these life transitions. However, depending on your situation, they will differ.

Because your place on the financial timeline is unique, you have your own set of goals that will change over the years. Maybe this will be the year you focus on your net worth, or it's all about positively changing your debt-to-income ratio.

If you have questions about achieving your financial goals, you will likely hear information from different sources. You will also likely hear information that does not apply to you or your situation.

When you go to the doctor with a question about improving your health, you will not get the same prescription the last patient received to make *you* feel better. It's the same thing when you want to improve your financial picture and lifestyle portfolio -- not everyone should receive the same prescription for their monetary health.

But finding the right financial choices for you starts with educating yourself about those choices and how to use them to your benefit. Only then can you be truly responsible for achieving the abundant life you want now and in the future.

FPN INNOVATION TEAM

Heading in the Right Financial Direction

When it comes to your finances, you may have heard that you should make this or that investment. You are told to follow one plan or another, and if you do not, all sorts of terrible things could happen. Far too often, here in the United States, we try to teach people through fear and intimidation.

On top of hearing all those possibilities for scary outcomes, your head may be spinning from hearing everything you should do from so many people, whether on social media or television.

Maybe you're hearing a plethora of conflicting advice that you don't even know if you're headed in the right financial direction anymore--or what that direction might be. And, of course, your financial direction can change over time, depending on where you are along your financial journey.

But instead of being concerned about or apprehensive of a financial outcome, what if you could be *empowered* to make informed, intelligent financial decisions that are right for you? What if you could have the kinds of discussions that will greatly enhance your awareness and assist you with making the choices you need to make now for the future you want?

I have coached and taught thousands of people to successfully grow their financial awareness--people like you.

This book is designed to teach you to become more aware of your choices and to decide which are the right ones

THE 8 FINANCIAL BREAKTHROUGHS

to achieve a real financial breakthrough and a successful future.

"It's simple arithmetic: Your income can grow only to the extent that you do."

T. Harv Eker

FPN INNOVATION TEAM

"Your economic security does not lie in your job; it lies in your own power to produce—to think, to learn, to create, to adapt. That's true financial independence. It's not having wealth; it's having the power to produce wealth."

Stephen Covey, educator, and author

Chapter 1

Building Financial Awareness (Breakthrough # 1)

Today, you can find more videos, social media posts, and financial self-help books than ever. However, they are all useless unless you can build the financial awareness necessary to understand your monetary picture.

Enhance your Financial Education

Understanding starts with knowledge that allows you to gain financial wisdom. That wisdom goes back to your roots. Perhaps you learned about money from your parents, grandparents, church, friends, or relatives.

No matter who taught you your first lessons about money, they undoubtedly greatly affected your financial habits. Some of the people you learned about money gave the advice they thought was best at the time. But others may have imparted true financial wisdom that goes beyond advice.

When someone gives you wisdom, they describe their mistakes, pitfalls, experiences, and wins. Unlike advice, which suggests or tells you what you should or must do, when someone shares a complete, well-rounded picture of their successes and failures, that's wisdom. Hearing about the good and bad will typically profoundly resonate with you because you are not just being told to "see the light," you are feeling the heat caused by actions or inaction. That kind of wisdom will help you achieve real financial knowledge.

"Most people don't change because they see the light, it's because they feel the heat."

Dr. Robert Anthony

THE 8 FINANCIAL BREAKTHROUGHS

Discover Your Financial DNA

Your financial DNA is what is programmed inside you. It is the wisdom that is imparted to you and the actions you see in your life from an early age.

It affects how you respond to the basics of finance and is deeply wired in you because of your heritage. For example, how your parents paid bills and unexpected expenses, which parent was in charge of making those payments, and what emotions they invoked when handling financial matters shape your financial DNA. You can trace your own reaction to your parents' and theirs to your grandparents. Financial DNA is so intrinsically a part of a person that you can see it passed down from generation to generation. And you may never understand or realize the reason behind the financial actions your DNA invokes.

There's an iconic story I like to share about baking a ham. A young girl (Tina) is watching her mother (Pam) prepare a ham for baking. The mother (Pam) cuts off both ends of the ham and throws them away, leaving about two thirds left. Her daughter (Tina) asks her why she cut the ham like that, as everything looked nice. Her mother (Pam) just shrugs and says that was what her mother did, but she thinks it helps with the juices. If her daughter wants to know why, she should ask her grandmother (Mattie Mae).

So, the girl goes to her grandmother (Mattie Mae). Grandma was, baking a ham. Just like her daughter (Pam), the grandmother (Mattie Mae) cuts off both ends of the ham before placing the larger piece in a pan for baking. The young girl (Tina) asks her why she (Mattie Mae) did that, and she was not sure of the reason either. Her (Mattie Mae) response was that's the way it has always been done. But, since the granddaughter (Tina) wants to know, she will ask her mother, Big Mama (Lucille).

The girl's grandmother (Mattie Mae) calls her own mama (Lucille) and asks her why she had always cut off the ends of the ham before baking it. Big Mama (Lucille) replies with a simple reason, one she would never be asked before: "The pan I had to use was too small."

How these multiple generations handled a ham is how we often handle money. We do not always know the reason we do things. Just as these women had no idea why they only baked a third of a ham, we often have no idea why we handle our money the way we do.

Family Financial Wisdom

While some people have ingrained financial habits that are passed from generation to generation without anyone knowing why, there are others whose families simply never share any financial information at all.

THE 8 FINANCIAL BREAKTHROUGHS

One of my recent clients came from a family that, for at least three generations, never shared any information about financial responsibilities or discussed money. That silence continued a lack of financial awareness for decades.

On the other hand, my family imparted many big and small financial ideas. Some were important, and some were small and even a bit quirky.

My mother told us to keep a little stash of money for our use that no one else knew about. She and her sisters did that. My father knows such a stash exists, but not what is in it.

My parents showed me by their actions that we could talk about money while sitting at the kitchen table.

Financial matters did not intrude on the dinner hour. That is a valuable idea that allows family meals to proceed without any financial stress interfering. However, they also passed on more significant elements of financial wisdom to me.

My father worked for the government in the post office and received paychecks every two weeks. Around the time I turned 10, he showed us his checks and explained things like overtime pay and taxes. He also told us how much money it took to provide for a family. I wish all kids were shown those things and gained awareness from an early age. It primed me to ask the adults questions about money.

Sometimes, I was the annoying kid asking adults how they could afford to pay for a new car, but that kind of awareness paid off for me. Because my father shared his financial information with me, I gained positive financial awareness about earning money and what things cost.

My mother was a public-school educator. But, unlike my dad, she was paid just once a month. From her experience, I learned about differences in payment times and supplementing income. My mother sold Avon beauty products to make extra money for Christmas presents, back-to-school shopping, and birthdays, as well as to avoid debts so many incurred on these occasions. I heard all my parents' stories and absorbed their wisdom. All of it contributed to a shared, collective financial awareness and empowerment.

Sure, you may pick up negative things as part of your financial DNA. But you may also have been given positive knowledge, which I was fortunate to receive.

If your family did not give you this knowledge, you likely got some financial basics from your first paycheck. I'm sure we all have that very first paycheck in common. And with that paycheck comes the experience of seeing all these amounts coming out of what you earned, such as Social Security, Medicare, and FICA payments. Seeing those deductions elevates your financial awareness!

But why are you surprised about those kinds of deductions in the first place? Typically, it is because you were not aware of them unless you were lucky enough to have a dad like mine who showed you his paycheck and explained everything to you as a kid.

We did not learn about those things in school. We were not taught about the deluge of credit card offers we typically receive as soon as we graduate from high school or college and the discipline, we need to avoid all the spending impulses placed in front of us. Instead, many books and seminars teach us about impossible things, like saving your way to great wealth. This imprints in your DNA, too.

Exploring Your Financial Type

Your financial DNA shapes what I think of as your financial type. There are essentially three types of people, financially speaking:

- Savers
- Spenders
- Avoiders

While spenders can overspend, the most dangerous financial type is the avoider. That's the person who doesn't open the mail when bills are due, refuses to acknowledge financial lacks, or refuses to invest in financial successes. If you are an avoider, you may simply not talk about it when things get hard financially instead of dealing with a situation. This can compound financial challenges for years to come.

If you are that type of person, you may be what I like to call a "**HENRY**– *high earner not rich yet*." Henrys think they will have lots of money coming in for the rest of their lives, with no awareness that money can stop anytime, whether from a lay-off, a shutdown, ill health, or for any other reason.

But no matter what financial type you may be, ask yourself where you picked up certain habits and how they became a part of you. You cannot correct bad habits until you've analyzed them and know where they came from in the first place.

It all comes back to gaining financial awareness, which is honestly one of the most important things we can do for financial success. Savers have their own need for education as well, not all saving is equally effective.

Financial Courses and Seminars

Along with the financial DNA that is embedded into us from an early age, many of us gain financial awareness by attending financial courses and seminars. This kind of learning is designed to help you understand the decisions you have made in the past and to help you become more aware of the types of decisions you want to make now and in the future.

THE 8 FINANCIAL BREAKTHROUGHS

After all, decisions impact you now and will also affect future generations. Making an educated decision are the keys to you and your family's future.

Former Business Consultant Jim Rohn said, "A formal education will make you a living; self-education will make you a fortune." Knowledge and education lead to making the right decisions.

As I have mentioned, many decisions are based on fear instead of empowerment. It seems as if everyone is offering financial advice, from social media influencers to seminars to family reunions and people at the barber shop or beauty salon. There is so much crazy advice out there. Far too many are designed to evoke an emotional response rather than provide a healthy conversation. However, what most people need to improve their financial awareness is to hear from someone whose financial wisdom aligns with their core beliefs. You need to hear someone encourage you to take an approach that fits you well.

In short, everyone needs someone who can provide a prescription for their specific financial health wellness needs. Let us start finding the right prescription for you.

"Money, like emotions, is something you must control to keep your life on the right track."

Natasha Munson

Homework

- How old were you when you got your first paycheck?
- How did you feel about the money you made back then?
- How have your perceptions about money changed?
- Who taught you your earliest lessons about money?
- Are there any habits they imparted that you still follow yourself?
- Did you hear about their mistakes and successes, or were you just told how you "should" do something?
- Are there any things you do financially that are just ingrained in you as a part of your financial DNA, things that you just do because you have always done them that way?
- Which of your financial habits would you change if you could? Why do you want to change them?
- Schedule a time with a financial professional.

THE 8 FINANCIAL BREAKTHROUGHS

"I'm always thinking about losing money as opposed to making money. Don't only focus on making money, focus on protecting what you have."

Paul Tudor Jones

Chapter 2

Protection

Threats from Loss of Income
(Breakthrough # 2)

    For most people, loss of income is a genuine threat. Yet far too few of us think about what we can do to protect ourselves from that threat.

    Let's look at it this way: You need insurance to stop a threat. Most likely, you have protection on your cell phone because, without it, you would not be able to communicate. You probably have car insurance to protect yourself and your vehicle in case you're in an accident. You most likely have homeowners' insurance to protect your home.

    In the same way, you need to protect yourself against a loss of income. You are your largest asset. Always protect your income today and any future income.

THE 8 FINANCIAL BREAKTHROUGHS

Ten Financial Threats

Consider these 10 significant financial threats and how you can protect yourself from them:

- **Losing income because of a disability is a significant financial risk.** Whether from injury or illness, disability insurance can protect you against income loss so you can continue receiving income even if you cannot work. Life insurance to protect your loved ones in the event of your passing is also essential.
- **Inflation** is a given. Think about how much you spend on simple items like a carton of milk over what you spent a few years ago. That same rate of inflation is affecting larger purchases and needs, such as buying an automobile, purchasing a home, or saving for retirement. You can protect yourself from inflation by making investments that stay ahead of it, like real estate or stocks. You could also consider investing in Treasury Inflation-Protected Securities, or TIPS. TIPS are treasury securities with principal and interest payments adjusted to account for inflation.
- **Running out of money** is a real concern during retirement. One of the best ways to protect yourself against this risk is by carefully planning to fund a

sustainable rate of withdrawal. You should also focus on making more diverse investments, providing increased security and stability for your investments during retirement.

- **Market downturns and losses** are other threats to address. One of the best ways to defend against these situations is with a diverse portfolio. Equally important is regularly reviewing and rebalancing your investments. By doing so, you can make sure you are meeting your financial goals and successfully manage your tolerance for risk, which may adjust over time.
- **Taxes** can also significantly affect your finances. Mitigation is critical and can be accomplished in several ways, including using tax-advantage strategies.

You should also plan to handle a rising tax rate. Taxes are almost inevitable to rise over time.

It is also important to be prepared if you receive an unexpected letter about additional taxes due or are subject to an audit. Can you sustain your financial security if either event occurs?

- **Identity theft** is another risk that is becoming increasingly common. Guard against it with unique and strong passwords. You should also monitor your financial accounts regularly to avoid any unauthorized activity. Identity theft protection services can offer you another robust level of security.

We live in a world of breaches, and security passwords are used on about everything to protect our good credit and every aspect of our lives. We have unbelievable information about ourselves on our cell phones alone. Keep that information safe. Do not share it with anyone you don't know or trust; secure it with passwords and monitoring.

- **Chronic illness**, like disability, can wreak havoc on your ability to earn and result in major health-care expenses. Long-term care insurance is one of the best ways to guard against these costs. This type of insurance can help with the expenses of assisted living, nursing home care, and in-home assistance.

Many people think they do not need this type of assistance. They believe someone in their family, such as their children or spouse, will step up and take care of them. But this can be difficult at best. Can you write down the names of five people who will stop everything to take care of you? Most of you cannot. But even if you could, do you really want your loved ones to be responsible for your daily care if you cannot take care of yourself? Long-term care insurance means you will not have to put your family in this position.

- **Critical illness**, such as cancer or heart disease, is another risk factor. Critical illness insurance provides a lump sum payable upon diagnosis to protect against the impact of critical illnesses on your finances.
- **Incorrect information** can also be a major financial risk. Make sure any financial advice comes from a trustworthy source, such as a certified financial planner, rather than an unreliable source.
- **Procrastination** can also be a significant threat to your financial well-being. Delaying planning or decisions can mean lost opportunities and savings. You can protect against this risk by setting goals, creating a timeline with manageable steps that work for you, and reviewing and adjusting your financial plan as needed.

These strategies will help protect your income and create a secure financial future.

Living Benefits

Guarding against financial threats means having living benefits to protect you and your family. I know a man who purchased insurance just 10 days before a car accident that permanently disabled him. He had been initially reluctant to buy insurance, thinking the cost was not necessary. Fortunately, he was persuaded otherwise. After his accident,

THE 8 FINANCIAL BREAKTHROUGHS

he was unable to work and initially required a great deal of costly care. Had he not had living benefits insurance, his family would not have been able to afford their mortgage or monthly expenses. He would not have had the care he needed to become more stable.

There are so many cautionary tales. If you are disabled or become seriously ill, you need to have protection for these situations. The unexpected can happen at any time. But rather than denying or worrying about this type of event, you must protect yourself and your family.

We all fear different threats, from death and disability to serious illness. Having living benefits to protect you will go a long way to eliminate your fears and financial risks when an impact on your health or safety occurs.

I've survived cancer twice. During my senior year in college, I received a diagnosis of fibrosarcoma when I thought all I had was a spider bite. At that time, I did not have a living benefit in place. **But I knew it could recur, so I decided to purchase the benefits that could protect me.** So, when I did experience a recurrence, I had the benefits I needed. When I needed surgery, I was able to use money from my life insurance policy to pay my bills for four months while I recovered. Without that financial support and peace of mind, my situation would have been more difficult.

Defense First

Remember, we all feel that a situation like this cannot happen to us; that's just human nature. But we are not invincible; it can happen to you or someone close to you.

It is essential to accept that it can happen and defend yourself against this situation. You might make the excuse that you are perfectly healthy, or you're too young to need this kind of insurance, or there are other things you want to spend your money on.

But creating protection for yourself from loss of income is vital. Why? Because we do not know when a threat can occur. What will happen to your family or business if something happens to you?

If you are the oldest or most responsible sibling, you will have a great deal of responsibility to care for your family, making having protection from financial threats even more essential. And getting that protection is as simple as finding the time to do so. Often, people do not make the time. Don't let that be you!

Protecting and defending yourself, your loved ones and your business from financial threats is the best defense against risk.

THE 8 FINANCIAL BREAKTHROUGHS

"I'd say it's that most people think that very wealthy people take huge risks and that's why they have huge rewards. But the very best on earth are completely obsessed with not losing money. That sounds overly simplistic, but they know that if you lost 50 percent, it takes 100 percent to get even. Most people don't make that math in their head, so it takes years and years. They are obsessed with not losing money."

Tony Robbins

FPN INNOVATION TEAM

Homework

- Are you taking steps to protect yourself against financial threats?
- Which threats concern you the most?
- If you were to become disabled or critically ill, can you name five people who would take care of you?
- Who are the three people who will stop everything and provide you with long-term care assistance?
- What kinds of living benefits would best serve to protect you?
- Which benefits would most positively affect you?

THE 8 FINANCIAL BREAKTHROUGHS

"There is really only one way to address cash flow crunches, and it's planning so you can prevent them in advance."

Elaine Pofeldt

Chapter 3
Considering Your Cash Flow Needs
(Breakthrough # 3)

Thinking about your cash flow needs is more paramount today than ever before. It's essential to pay attention to the flow of cash coming in.

People often focus on reducing their expenses when managing their budgets, opting to cut bills. However, without increasing their cash flow, this approach may not be effective. To truly succeed in managing your finances and ensuring stability for yourself and your family, you need a cash flow enhancement plan.

Understanding your cash flow needs is essential for financial planning. It involves tracking income and expenses to ensure you have enough money to cover your bills, save for the future, and achieve your financial goals.

THE 8 FINANCIAL BREAKTHROUGHS

Cash Flow Is Your Ace

Think of your cash flow as the **ACE** in your financial hand of cards. Your cash is **KING**, and credit is your **QUEEN**.

You'll do fine if you have excellent cash flow, even if you don't yet have your king of cash and queen of credit. Financial success always starts with cash flow.

On the other hand, if you only have that queen of credit, you can't be successful with only that part of your financial hand. If you depend solely on your credit for financing, that credit will go bad quickly.

Similarly, even if you have a large sum of your cash king, if you don't have a steady cash flow, that initial cash amount will likely start dwindling too soon.

In your financial card game, it's good to have all three components of a winning hand: your ace, king, and queen. When you have all three, there's a good chance you'll win, no matter what financial game you may be playing.

Having only a cash **(KING)** or credit **(QUEEN)** in hand does not guarantee a winning hand. Even having both of those combined is not a guarantee.

But if you have that **ACE** – your cash flow – you can end up with a win.

FPN INNOVATION TEAM

Your Daily Income Goal (D.I.G)

How do you receive the cash flow you need to win a financial game? The most crucial step in watching and enhancing your cash flow is establishing your daily income goal also known as **D.I.G** Think about it for a minute. What is your daily income goal for today?

Whatever your regular income may be, there is a great deal of power in having an additional income number you want to hit, whether that goal is having an extra $1,000 each month in income, $10,000, or whatever that number may be. The point is to have a *daily* goal, write it down, and don't alter it.

Consider what that additional amount could mean for you or your family. It may mean that you can purchase a house instead of renting. It could also mean you can fix your car's air conditioner. Perhaps you can help put your children through college, or you can take a family vacation. Whatever that extra amount might mean, visualize that purpose, and then consider what opportunities you could take advantage of to achieve your goal.

In short, have a cash flow enhancement plan because today, more than ever, you need to rely on more than a single income stream to succeed.

Consider the lifestyle you desire--from the car you want to drive to the house you want to live in and the places you

THE 8 FINANCIAL BREAKTHROUGHS

want to eat. How could you enhance your cash flow to achieve this lifestyle? How much monthly cash flow will transform your lifestyle?

You must rely on yourself to improve your **D.I.G.** To a large extent, having a consistent paycheck with a retirement plan provided by your company is a thing of the past. Adding an extra gig or two is necessary to have more cash flow. That could be anything from taking surveys online to earning extra cash or gift cards or investing in real estate. For my mom, it was selling her Avon products.

Chris, 30, and Lisa, 27, are married. They're childless, but Chris's parents, who are 62 and 65, are retired on a fixed income and living with them. Chris works for Delta Airlines, making $52,000 annually. Lisa works for Google and earns $112,000 a year. They have a 15-year mortgage of $450,000, which costs them $3,400 per month. They have $7,000 in credit card debt. Chris has $65,000 in his 401K, and Lisa has $90,000 in hers. They want to pay off their home and start a family, which will mean that Lisa may cut back on some of her work hours, reducing her salary. Will cutting back on expenses, such as economizing on their grocery bill and canceling their cable television subscription, help them to achieve their goals? No, what they need to do is increase their cash flow.

An increase in cash flow is also what would make a real difference for 40-year-old Jason and 44-year-old Carmen.

FPN INNOVATION TEAM

Jason's accounting firm recently downsized, and he's currently driving for Uber. Carmen works for the IRS and earns $58,000. They have four children: 3, 5, 10, and 16. Together, they have $10,000 in their checking and savings accounts and are $37,000 in debt. Their mortgage is $1,850 a month for a $320,000 mortgage. Jason has $20,000 in his 401K, and Carmen has $90,000 in a TSP (Thriving Savings Plan) that is available for federal employees. Their budget is already stretched to the breaking point. They are not even sure what they would cut from their expenses if they could.

My point is that for both these families, having more cash flow coming in is important. *Making more income is more important than cutting your budget.*

You won't increase your cash flow by cutting coupons and curtailing any activity that costs money. Instead, you should focus on how you could be making an extra $500 a month instead of trying to save $50 a month.

It's crucial to develop a mindset of abundance and focus on growth rather than budgeting, which can potentially have a negative effect on growing your wealth. Instead of thinking of ways to constrain and contain yourself and your spending, focus on how you can expand your cash flow. Quit focusing on what you're saving and start focusing on what you're growing.

THE 8 FINANCIAL BREAKTHROUGHS

Shift your narrative to increasing cash flow instead of focusing on your budget or debts.

You can't increase your cash flow and wealth by trimming your budget until there is nothing else to cut. Nothing will improve your financial picture if you don't set a goal for extra money and start earning it—whether it is $100 or $1,000. Set a goal to increase your cash flow and take control of your finances. Make a financial promise to yourself and keep it.

For Jason and Carmen, starting a business venture, perhaps in Jason's prior field of accounting, could be key. For Chris and Lisa, perhaps Lisa can best utilize her skills as a consultant for other companies, increasing the amount of money she brings home when she cuts back on her regularly scheduled working hours.

Unnecessary Expenses

While not applicable to these two couples, there may be some unnecessary expenses that you can eliminate. We all have small costs that add up and may be causing a little leak in your financial boat.

For example, is there an automatic draft that comes out of your bank account every month that you meant to terminate but did not? Perhaps it's a second gym membership or an extra movie streaming service you never or rarely watch. Whatever it may be, getting rid of a forgotten or disregarded expense is always a good idea.

Addressing Your Major Money Concerns

Like everyone else, you highly likely have three major money concerns:

- Will I run out of money?
- Will I lose money?
- How do I make more money?

As important as these are, I also encourage you to consider how much money you will need to transform your lifestyle monthly.

But it all starts with improving your cash flow, enhancing your cash flow today until it becomes tomorrow's new, improved cash flow.

As businessman and philanthropist David Tang says:

"The three most dreaded words in the English language are 'negative cash flow.'"

THE 8 FINANCIAL BREAKTHROUGHS

Increasing Your Zero

When considering your cash flow needs, the bottom line is *increasing your zero*.

Increasing your zero means establishing an amount you will not dip below in your bank account. Over time, that amount should increase. Some people consider their zero to be when the bank sends an overdrawn account notice and assesses a $35 fee to cover it. Others set their zero at $1,000, $10,000, or even $100,000 of liquid capital.

Every year, you should raise the bar on your financial zero. Keep raising your bar and working to achieve your new goal. I put this idea into practice when I was 23 years old. I consistently apply it as a financial discipline today.

When you establish a new, ever-increasing "zero," you won't feel right if you're in danger of dropping below that number. You'll work hard to keep improving your cash flow to ensure you don't drop below that number. Keep moving that floor up every year and look for the opportunities that allow you to do so.

"Making more money will not solve your problems if cash flow management is your problem."

Robert Kiyosaki

Homework

- What is your D.I.G. or daily income goal?
- Can you think of ways in which you can support that goal?
- Are you shifting your financial narrative from increasing your cash flow instead of focusing on budgeting and reducing expenses?
- What steps can you take to do so?
- How do you think making this change in your financial thinking could benefit you?
- What is your "zero" that you won't let your bank account drop below? What can you do to increase your zero?
- Are you open to increasing your cash flow?

THE 8 FINANCIAL BREAKTHROUGHS

"Worrying is like paying on a debt that may never come due."

Will Rogers

Chapter 4

Debt-to-Income Ratio

It's Time to Stop Viewing Debt as a Monster
(Breakthrough # 4)

So many people worry about debt. They view the very idea of debt as a big, bad monster. But there is a way to think about debt more positively. Instead of being terrified by it, you can deal with it.

Usually, debt isn't something you really think about until you decide to buy a house, rent an apartment, or purchase a car. When you make a big purchase, you start worrying about the debt you've taken on. It becomes a big weight that often seems frightening, yet you can't avoid it. There are three main important aspects to consider regarding your debt-to-income ratio:

- First, manage your debt and liabilities.
- Second, improve your cash flow awareness.
- Third, increase your credit score.

Managing Your Debt--It's Not Always a Liability

Let's start with that first point: managing your debt and liability. It's important to manage your debt and, in doing so, consider your debt-to-income ratio, which means your debts and liabilities. Many people see debts and liabilities as the same thing, but they are not.

Your debt-to-income ratio is your monthly debt payments divided by your monthly income. In short, your DTI compares how much you owe monthly to how much you earn. It's the percentage of your monthly income before taxes to pay your rent, mortgage, credit card bills, or other debt. Lenders look at this ratio to see if you can manage the payments on a debt.

If you want to be debt-free and pay off your debts, you should consider the number if you were to pay off your car or your house today. Considering this kind of knowledge helps you keep an eye on your debt. With that knowledge, you will see how your debt-to-income ratio will affect your purchasing power.

In many cases, it's not your credit score or the lack of a down payment that stops you from purchasing your dream house—it's your debt-to-income ratio **(DTI)**.

Think about it the same way you look at the amount of fuel you have in your gas tank. You cannot effectively keep driving your car if the low fuel light comes on. So, to keep driving, you will want to refill your tank, maybe when you're no lower than having a quarter tank.

Your debt-to-income ratio **(DTI)** works in the same way. You want to fill up the "tank" of your income to keep your debt, or gas use, in check. You need to increase your monthly income to improve the percentage of that income you retain after paying your debts.

Cash Flow Awareness
Cash Flow Is Still Your Ace

Remember that your cash flow will always be the ace in your financial card game. You do not want to use up all the cash you have or live off your credit cards.

Of course, many entrepreneurs start their businesses living off credit until their new income flows in. Maybe that credit is a bank loan, or you are using your credit cards to get by while establishing your business. Likewise, you may have to use your credit until you start a new position if you're unemployed.

These aren't necessarily bad situations; they develop when you transition. But you can't let these situations last for a long time. You need to get your cash flow in as soon as possible to manage your debt-to-income ratio.

The Difference Between Liability and Debt

Sometimes, the fear of taking on a large debt can stop you from acting, even if that action benefits you in the long term.

One way to prevent inaction is to recognize that *a debt is not always a liability*, even though many people confuse the two. However, there's a big difference between them.

For example, if your car has one problem after another that drains you financially, that's a liability. Maybe it needs new brakes one month and has an oil leak the next. Perhaps it's an older car that constantly breaks down when you need it for important business or family matters. If that is the case, as well as costing you in repairs, it's costing you time and affects your business and personal life.

When one of these situations sounds familiar, it becomes clear that you need a new car. You'll get into debt to buy that new car because you must borrow money. The idea of taking on debt may be frightening to you. But if you let that fear stop you from purchasing a new car, you're stuck with an old car that's always breaking down and has become a liability.

Many people fear debt. They are not afraid of the monthly debt payment, but of the overall large debt they're taking on.

But you need to consider that no creditor will knock on your door at night and ask you to repay the amount you borrowed. Creditors just want you to keep making the monthly payment on that debt.

Maybe you're considering returning to school instead of getting a new car. To do so, you need a student loan. That school loan amount may seem impossible if you consider it a lump sum of $50,000.

Instead, try looking at that student loan amount as a $200 monthly payment to help you achieve what you want to achieve rather than as a total sum. Viewed in this way, it's far less daunting. Do not let the large debt prevent you from getting what you need.

Instead, you need to consider whether you can service your debt every month rather than the overall amount of the debt.

THE 8 FINANCIAL BREAKTHROUGHS

Debt Is a Part of Cash Flow

Here's one way to look at debt: as a part of your cash flow. Of course, it's not the cash flow coming in, but it *is* a part of the cash flow going out. Over time, you can eliminate your debt. But remember, you should be focusing on increasing the cash flow you have coming in rather than on decreasing your debts and the cash flow going out. But do both!

Good Debt and Bad Debt

You should also be aware of both good and bad debt in your financial life. Understanding the difference between these two types of debt is a part of good debt-to-income management.

A good debt may be your first line of credit, for example. Because everyone needs a credit profile, you want to start your credit history as early as possible. My credit history began with the Capital One card I received right out of college. As long as you pay your credit card bills on time, you are enhancing your debt-to-income ratio, not lowering it.

A good debt could also be the amount you incur when buying that new car to replace your old vehicle when it becomes a liability.

Even though buying that new car is a good debt, it could easily become bad. If you purchase a pricy luxury vehicle you do not need rather than a reliable one, that's a bad debt. In that case, you have taken on a larger than necessary loan for a car that will be more expensive to maintain and a vehicle you do not need in the first place.

It is the same thing with buying a house. A good debt is taking on that house payment so that you do not have to pay rent every month, rent that could rise at any time. Incurring a home loan to do so is a good debt. But that home loan becomes a bad debt if you buy a bigger, fancier house than you can afford. Now, you have no money left to furnish it, or your cash flow can't handle the payments without straining your bank account.

Remember,

A good debt allows you to live within your means; a bad debt just increases your debt.

In short, it's a good debt if you have the cash flow necessary to pay off your debt and a plan to do so. If taking on a debt helps you get the education you need to get work and improve your cash flow, that's a good debt.

After all, the improved income you'll earn from your education will allow you to pay off the money you owe to finance that education.

Here's another example of a good debt: you incur a debt to make an investment that will increase in value and generate cash flow.

Conversely, if you have no plan to pay off your debt and your cash flow is too limited to allow you to do so, that's a bad debt.

The bottom line is this:

If taking on a debt doesn't serve or help you in life, that is a bad debt.

Increasing Your Credit Score

Be aware of debt and when it's good and bad for you to take on. This awareness will help you increase your credit score and improve your debt-to-income ratio.

No matter what you see on TV or hear on the Internet about the importance of becoming debt-free, that is not the key to your financial success. Knowing and improving your debt-to-income ratio is what's key.

Knowing your debt-to-income ratio is crucial for assessing your financial health and understanding how much of your income is going towards debt repayment. Improving your debt-to-income ratio can involve increasing income, reducing debt, or a combination of both, leading to better financial stability and creditworthiness.

Find the correct answers for you personally to questions like these:

- How can you improve your debt-to-income number?
- How can taking on debt but increasing your cash flow help increase your credit score?

Those are the essential questions you should be asking and the answers you should be looking for, not how to become entirely debt-free.

My family bought new cars when they needed them. They were not impulse buys. My dad would get a low-interest loan from his credit union and use that loan to buy a new ride. Yes, he was taking on debt to do so. But he made the payments on time and had the necessary vehicle to keep working and serve our family. He did not purchase the type of luxury vehicle that he could not afford. His credit improved right along with his cash flow. Each time he went through this process, successfully paying off his car loan, his credit score improved. Because of that, he was able to get better loans. A positive credit score will save you and make you and your family more money.

THE 8 FINANCIAL BREAKTHROUGHS

Addressing the Emotion of Debt

Even if you can see that taking on debt isn't necessarily bad, there are still negative emotions associated with debt.

Society has ingrained those emotions in us. But just as it's important to focus on improving your cash flow instead of trimming your budget, it's important to shift your focus to debt.

Instead of thinking of debt as this big, bad monster that will devour you, focus on increasing your debt-to-income ratio.

To grow financially, we must change our language about money. That includes changing the language we use regarding debt. You should think about how debt can benefit you in the future rather than worrying about it somehow causing you to lack in the present.

"Bad debt is sacrificing your future day needs for your present-day desires."

Suze Orman

Homework

- Do you know the difference between good debt and bad debt?
- Can you name some examples of taking on a good debt and what that might mean for you?
- What is the difference between liability and debt?
- What liabilities do you have?
- Do you know your debt-to-income ratio?
- What could you do to improve it?
- Do you have a debt freedom date (DFD)?

THE 8 FINANCIAL BREAKTHROUGHS

"Liquidity equals freedom."

Hendrith Vanlon Smith Jr.

Chapter 5

Liquidity
(Breakthrough # 5)

The freedom of liquidity cannot be overemphasized. Having sufficient liquid capital is essential to a healthy financial picture overall.

Your liquidity is tied to the important cash flow enhancement plan discussed previously. Multiple income streams are crucial to your liquidity today and a strong financial future.

Focus on What You're Growing

Focusing on the income you're growing instead of the money you're saving puts your financial energy into the most favorable place.

THE 8 FINANCIAL BREAKTHROUGHS

We spend too much energy and time saving a dollar here and there instead of putting that time and energy toward creating another source of cash flow. Do not waste your time clipping coupons. Focusing on new sources of income will not only provide you with a more abundant lifestyle, but it will also allow you to have more options in life overall.

Many of our parents saw some aspect of the Great Depression in their parents or grandparents. Over the generations, we have absorbed some of that behavior in which every dollar matters greatly. Even though today's lifestyle and earning capabilities are different from during the Depression, it is all too easy to maintain that "every penny saved is a penny earned" mentality.

Cash Flow Enhancement Plan

However, rather than pinching pennies, the best way to grow liquidity is to have a *cash flow enhancement plan*.

What that may entail is really any way to create extra money for yourself and your family. It could be from an entrepreneurial activity, a second job, a random marketing opportunity, savvy investments, or getting a promotion.

The point is you need to obtain more income streams and increase your liquidity by creating more money rather than saving those precious dollars here and there.

The Emotional Circumstances of Earning

The circumstances surrounding how you earn money are another thing to bear. How you earn affects your emotions regarding that money. Pay attention to how your emotions can change based on how you receive an income stream and enhance your liquidity.

Let's say I owe you $100. When you see me out and about, you ask me to pay you back, and I will give you that $100. That feels different emotionally than if I simply gave you $100 as a gift.

It's also a different feeling from earning $100 working together. Likewise, it would feel different if we were to fight over $100 and whether I owed it to you to pay that amount.

The highest level of emotion is usually reserved for a circumstance in which someone takes money from you or when you need to access your money and can't.

Whether you find $100 lying on the ground, take $100, or find an additional, unexpected charge or hold on your credit card for $100, each of these circumstances creates an entirely different emotion, too.

These varying emotions all tie in with the ingrained mentality of saving a $1 here and there. Emotion drives out the logic for people who absorb that older idea about saving over the importance of growth and expanded liquidity.

THE 8 FINANCIAL BREAKTHROUGHS

The current generation and their children have received so many more material items and have so much more access to money than our parents, or perhaps more than we did ourselves. For younger generations, it's easier to see the importance of growth and its reason—to establish new income streams and develop greater liquidity.

When you have more than one income stream, you're also adding to your financial security. You'll find yourself capable of saving without limiting your growth. You can use one source of income solely for saving and another for spending.

Every Pile of Money Needs a Job

Once you've enhanced your cash flow, it's a solid idea to create multiple accounts—one for each income stream. Organize your money into separate "buckets" for use.

Essentially, you're "hiring" your money to perform the job indicated by the bucket you place in it. You can organize your spending by type of bank account, such as fun spending, vacation account, emergency account, or investment account.

In our house, we nickname our bank accounts, such as "Vacation Spot" or "Debt Freedom Account." Whenever I do accounting, I also make sure that I indicate the names of these separate buckets. I always give my money an assigned job, so it doesn't just get piled into one lump account. Doing this helps you to know exactly how much you have available for each specific use. Every bucket of money is needed to do the job you assign to it.

Prepare a 6 to 12-Month Emergency Fund

One job you should always assign to one bucket is that of an "Emergency Fund." Having 6 to 12 months of emergency funding available will make your life much easier.

Think about how you handled your last emergency. Did you need to call your parents or another family member? Did you have to deal with your emergency by putting the costs on a credit card? Or did you have an emergency fund in place?

If you did, you were prepared to manage the situation, whatever it may have been, without affecting others in your family or incurring new and unwanted debt.

It's always a good idea to ask yourself these questions:

- Are you prepared for an emergency? What does being prepared for an emergency mean to you?
- Do you rely on your credit cards to cover an emergency?
- What was your largest emergency regarding the liquidity you needed to deal with?

Let's take a closer look at these questions. We've all had emergencies. Some are simply more costly than others. For example, what if your water heater failed and flooded your house? What if there was a major illness in your family? Or you had to fly to a distant location to deal with a family health issue, front the cost of emergency care, and pay for a hotel stay and food for a month or more? None of these situations are uncommon, and each is a definite emergency.

Of course, some people think an emergency is a situation where they simply run out of money while working on a project. An acquaintance recently told me they needed $27,000 to complete construction on a new vacation home and needed the money immediately. They asked me if I could be of assistance. But a situation like that is a failure of planning, not a true emergency. Just because your emotions rise because of an immediate need doesn't make your situation an emergency, which should affect me.

Do You Have the Liquidity to Handle Emergency Situations?

It's well worth considering whether your capital is primarily tied up in your home or if you have liquidity available and earmarked for emergencies.

You never know when having actual cash in hand could become necessary to deal with an emergency. That being said, I recommend having at least two months of a six-month emergency fund available in cash.

If you cannot earmark that kind of liquidity, it can be difficult to manage should an emergency occur. As important as having available cash is, most people refuse to acknowledge the possibility of this kind of need.

They deny the possibility that an emergency could occur or resist the idea that if one should happen, they would not be able to handle it. They fully believe that should such a situation occur, they would somehow get the help they need, even if they don't recognize the possibility in the first place.

There's a classic story about a storm that floods a town with rain and a swollen river. One man is perched on his rooftop as the water rises.

At that moment, a boat came by, and the rowing team said they were there to save that fellow on the rooftop. But the man stayed on the rooftop and refused to go. "I'm good," he said.

Next, a helicopter came, and hovered overhead. The pilot shouted through a megaphone that he was there to save the man on the roof, but the man said he was good because God was watching out for him, and he knew he'd be fine.

Finally, the Navy SEALs came through, offering to rescue the man, but he still refused. He said the Lord was watching over him no matter what.

THE 8 FINANCIAL BREAKTHROUGHS

But sure enough, the flood waters continued to rise, and the man drowned.

When he went to Heaven, he said, *"God, why didn't you help me? I believed you'd always be there to help and save me."*

Well, God just looked at him and shook His head.

He said, *"Man, I sent you a boat, a helicopter, and even Navy SEALs. And you turned them all down."*

Unfortunately, that's how many people act when they're confronted with the idea of an emergency. Instead of using the various potential liquidity rescues they have available, they ignore the possibility of a tough situation even happening.

It's as if they were standing at the top of Niagara Falls, and the ground was slipping away. But instead of returning from the brink, they believe the ground would stabilize somehow. They simply don't see the drop in front of them or ignore that their fall is just waiting to happen.

I'm trying to shine a light where that light needs to shine. Preparing for an emergency is essential, and your preparation goal should always be to have a bucket of money earmarked for emergency use only--not money commingled

FPN INNOVATION TEAM

with funds you want for a vacation or to take advantage of earning opportunities.

Remember, nothing beats having cash and available funds for emergencies.

"Money is good. And the more, the better."

Hendrith Vanlon Smith Jr.

THE 8 FINANCIAL BREAKTHROUGHS

Homework

- Do you have an emergency fund in place?
- If an emergency should occur, how would you handle it?
- What kind of cash flow enhancement plan could you create to increase your current and future liquidity?
- Do you have multiple accounts to support different needs?
- Schedule a time with a financial professional.

FPN INNOVATION TEAM

"You have no value if you have no liquidity."

Sam Zell

Chapter 6

Liquidity and Opportunity

A 12-month plan for business opportunities is just as important a money bucket as a six-month emergency fund. Why is an opportunity fund so important? It's vital because you need access to capital and funding, so you won't miss out on opportunities to grow your wealth when they arise.

If you don't have that kind of access and a 12-month opportunity plan, you're missing out on many ways to enhance your cash flow.

Preparing a 12-Month Plan for Opportunities

Have you ever had a business opportunity but lacked the capital to take advantage of it?

You may also have been overlooked for business opportunities because you could not take advantage of the last two opportunities you were presented with.

If neither of those situations suits you, perhaps this one will. Have you ever missed the opportunity to join your friends or family on a nice vacation because you lacked liquid capital?

Any of these situations can occur all too easily if you do not have a 12-month liquidity plan to take advantage of potential opportunities.

Unfortunately, not having available capital is familiar to me. On one past occasion, I had a terrific opportunity presented to me to invest in a hotel project. But I did not have the liquid cash available to put toward it. The result was that I missed out on a ground-floor opportunity that easily generated a great deal of cash flow for those who could participate.

Just like that all-important emergency liquidity, you need some liquidity available to pursue the opportunities in your life.

You cannot do that if your money is tied up in nonliquid assets. This can be a common situation, especially for business owners with a lot invested in brick-and-mortar businesses.

You won't be very liquid if all your capital is tied up in new computers or office furniture. But while these kinds of business investments and costs may appear to make a lot of

THE 8 FINANCIAL BREAKTHROUGHS

sense to you, the truth is that when you have liquid cash available:

- You'll make decisions that are better for you and your future.
- You'll make decisions that will improve and grow your cash flow.
- You can build different relationships when you have liquid cash in hand versus when you have no liquidity available.

Cash is the most liquid asset because you can convert it far more rapidly in any number of opportunities than you can with other assets. These assets—like computers or furnishings—are intangible and far less liquid. If you have cash in intangible assets, buildings, or other real estate, you won't be able to convert them quickly.

Remember, liquidity means you can convert an asset you have into cash without losing any money. The easier it may be for you to turn an asset into cash money, then the more liquid that asset is.

If you're a real estate investor, and you have all your money tied up in property that's valuable for the future, that doesn't make you liquid. And even if those property investments will appreciably grow in value in the future, tying up all your funds in this way makes you less safe in the present.

Let's unpack that idea:

If you do not have any cash because your money is all tied up in assets that you can't easily make liquid, even if you feel your future is assured, you're not safe in the here and now.

Having your money locked up in nonliquid assets can cause your present-day debt to get out of hand and your cash flow to fall into disarray.

Let's say you own a fleet of cars or trucks. They're valuable assets, but they are not liquid. Suppose someone you trust offers you the opportunity to invest in a great house if you join a team of other investors. Each investor only needs to put $100,000 into the house, and then you can flip it and double your money in six months. Unfortunately, you won't be able to invest because you don't have the liquidity to do so.

Without maintaining some liquidity, you'd be trying to scrape up the money, and very likely, you'd fail to do so in a timely enough period to take part in the offered investment. Even if you make an investment in an opportunity that doesn't turn out as well as you wanted, losing out on the ability to be a part of an opportunity can cost you in the long run.

THE 8 FINANCIAL BREAKTHROUGHS

You may feel desperate to participate in opportunities you miss because you're not liquid. You'll likely start to show that desperation; honestly, people can sense it and won't approach you. Your desperation then adds to further lost opportunities.

Remember, if your money is invested in the future, you can't live off that money today. Without liquid capital, you can't take advantage of opportunities or handle the emergencies we've discussed.

If you run a business without liquidity, you may be unable to make your payroll, hire staff members, purchase supplies, or increase your inventory when needed. This is still the case even if you own the building where your business is.

Acquire Access to Capital and Funding

By now, you can see that liquidity is necessary for your well-being both now and in the future. If you don't have it, you need to acquire it.

There are many ways to access capital and funding. Remember, if you are holding a set of financial cards that include the ace of cash flow, the king of cash, and the queen of credit, things will go well for you. But without those resources, it is not going to work.

Your actual net worth involves the amount of money you have access to now.

So, if you don't have that liquid cash in hand, you could:

- Reach out to someone you have a relationship with to get cash. What type of relationship do you have with this person? Make sure this is not contradictory to something said earlier in the book.
- Approach your bank or another credit lending institution to get the cash you need.

Relationship Capital

If you work with business colleagues or have family or friends you can call on, perhaps you can ask them to wire $20,000 to take advantage of an opportunity or to improve your cash flow. Who knows these types of people? That's a way to ruin a relationship.

But to be able to do so, you need to work on establishing this kind of relationships. You can't just call someone out of the blue and ask for cash.

Your "word" should be reliable, and it's easier to gauge that when you know someone well. If people know your word is good, then it is likely that your relationship capital can bring you conversations about liquidity as well as new relationships. Both can help you improve your cash flow.

Barring relationship capital, you can contact banks and other lenders to gain liquidity. Of course, to do so, it is not just your word that has to be good--your credit needs to be good, too.

Learn How Banks Work and the Role They Play in Liquidity

Banks play a big part in the liquidity that buys you time and sustainability. Banking institutions report to the Federal Reserve how much money was deposited that day. If they have a certain amount deposited each day, then they can lend that money to others. Normally, the ratio is 10 to 1.

What is a bank reserve ratio?

In the United States, the Federal Reserve dictates the amount of cash, called the reserve ratio, that each bank must maintain. Historically, the reserve ratio has ranged from zero to 10 percent of bank deposits. Bank reserves are the minimal amounts of cash that banks must keep on hand in case of unexpected demand.

Banks control liquidity to a substantial extent. They use their own form of credit, just as you can. For example, Susan had $30,000 in cash in the bank and a $30,000 limit on her American Express card.

When her business struggled and times grew hard, she needed an infusion of liquidity to enhance her cash flow. She decided that the best way to get it was to spend the money she had available on her American Express card before she spent the cash money, she had in her own bank account. When she spent the amount, she had available as a cash advance on her American Express card, she bought herself some time.

She could make small payments on the amount that she borrowed for a few months until her business cash flow improved. In that way, the liquidity of her credit bought her three or four months of sustainability and opportunity.

More than anything else, *liquidity should buy you time*. Banks know that and act on it. You can, too. Even in otherwise chaotic times, if you have liquid money, you can take advantage of opportunities such as low-cost stocks, even when others are becoming afraid.

You can take advantage of any opportunity when you have liquidity available, whether cash, credit, or relationship capital.

After all, when times are hard, people can become desperate to rid themselves of a property, whether that property involves collectible items like a prized Michael Jordan or Kobe Bryant collectible card or a Chevrolet Corvette. When times are tough, people sell their assets at a discount to regain their liquidity.

If you have opportunity liquidity, however, you can access capital, whether through cash, credit, private, or institutional money. Then you will get ahead.

Even if you are having difficulty maintaining cash flow, if you can access liquid capital through available credit, you can stay liquid. You can still retain your cash while taking advantage of whatever opportunities arise. You can achieve a real financial breakthrough by acting on this knowledge.

Having More Money at the End of The Month Instead of More Month Than Money

Liquidity is about having more money at the end of the month than you have days in the month. All too many people live in the opposite way and experience having more months than they have money.

Many people are forced to live off their credit cards at the end of the month. They may run out of money on the 20th, which is 10 days before they receive any more cash flow. But that is not the way you should live or how you should want to live.

Because your goal should always be having more money at the end of the month rather than having more months than money, you need to know how and where to acquire capital.

FPN INNOVATION TEAM

Some people may feel they have unlimited access to acquiring capital when, in fact, they do not. Perhaps they have unlimited access until the bank starts pulling their line of credit, their bank loan comes due, or their grandmother says she can't loan them any funds this month because she must repair her roof.

It is a privilege to have access to money, not a guarantee. If that privilege is taken away, you will quickly be in debt and out of commission.

Having good access to capital comes back to maintaining liquidity. When you maintain your liquidity, you will have access to cash, which you can depend on no matter the situation.

"It's liquidity that moves markets."

Stanley Druckenmiller

THE 8 FINANCIAL BREAKTHROUGHS

Homework

- Do you have liquid cash, or are your assets nonliquid?
- If your assets are not liquid, do you have a resource to use to get cash?
- If you do not have cash, what capital can you easily and quickly access?
- Do you have money left over at the end of each month, or do you have more days left when you have already run out of money?
- What can you do to reverse that situation in terms of your liquidity?
- How can you make your assets more liquid if you need to do so?

"All our dreams can come true, if we have the courage to pursue them."

Walt Disney

Chapter 7

Shaping Your Future Income
(Breakthrough # 6)

You are on a journey to build your desired income throughout your lifetime. That journey takes you from preparing to accumulate wealth to distributing it. It shapes how you think about your lifestyle now and in the future during retirement.

Accumulating and Growing Your Money

The first phase of your financial journey is accumulating money. Then comes growing it. Once you have grown your money, you need to decide the best way to receive and distribute it.

The amount of tax you are comfortable paying when you receive your money in the future is one decision you must make. Do you want taxable or tax-free income, even if a tax-free investment offers a smaller rate of return? Do you want a steady, fixed income, year after year, or do you want to live large off a lump sum of principal until it is gone?

What kind of life do you envision yourself living as you get older? There are many choices to be made when planning your future. For example, if you have the option to live off your post-work income and maintain your lifestyle, is that your goal?

It all comes down to how you see your future lifestyle unfolding.

Envisioning and Planning for Your Future

How do you envision your future lifestyle? Think about what you want and see yourself doing when you are no longer accumulating wealth.

Many people want to travel and explore new places, while others prefer to stay home. Is your future filled with exotic overseas travel? Do you want to buy an RV and travel domestically? Do you want to travel at all, or just spend more time with your family?

THE 8 FINANCIAL BREAKTHROUGHS

If you envision family time, how does that time unfold? Are you thinking about quiet family dinners, or do you want to host big family events?

Do you see yourself driving an electric car and owning the latest iPhone, or do you plan to live within walking distance of all your activities and play Bingo once a week?

Think about the lifestyle you want for your future! If you are on a journey to build a desired income, you need to have a picture in mind of what comes next after your accumulation phase.

Having a lifestyle plan is much more powerful than shaping what is commonly called a retirement plan.

Take control of your financial future today! In a world where financial stability can seem uncertain, having a tailored plan is not just an option—it is essential. Schedule a consultation with a seasoned financial professional to explore how you can secure a strong financial plan. Do not let another day pass you by. Are you comfortable with current your retirement plan?

Your financial future starts with a decision to take control. It is a commitment to learn, to plan, and to act. With each step, you pave the way toward financial security and freedom. Financial security means having the peace of mind that comes with knowing your basic needs are met and you have a buffer for unexpected expenses. Financial freedom goes beyond security, offering the ability to make choices based on your desires and goals, not just necessity.

Address What's Necessary for Your Lifestyle Plan

Naturally, your lifestyle plan should first address the basics, the acronym for which is **M.U.G**. Those letters refer to:

M - Mortgage Payment
U - Utilities
G - Groceries

Next comes getting a "**G.R.I.P.**" To do so, you need to consider your financial:

G – Growth
R – Reasonable Rate of Return
I – Income for Life
P – Principal Protection

You should consider the possibility of taking care of your parents or a special needs child, whether that means serving as a caregiver or paying for an appropriate care facility. In either case, this care will affect your finances and lifestyle.

THE 8 FINANCIAL BREAKTHROUGHS

Rising inflation should also be considered when planning your net worth. Your income needs to satisfy the future, and with the dollar's value decreasing, you need to ensure that your money keeps up with future inflation.

If you do not have enough income and are basing your future lifestyle on Social Security, keeping up with inflationary costs will be almost impossible. Inflation plays a significant role in your future.

To be secure despite inflation, you must be sure your money's growth beats inflation's cost yearly. You need to increase your net worth over time.

Make sure that your currency keeps moving forward and flowing in. The word currency itself connotes movement, and that is exactly what your money must do. It cannot just sit there; it must adjust to the rate of inflation and flow forward ahead of that rate.

The best way to build your net worth is to buy it through life insurance, property, trust, or any other means. As you create your net worth, you also need to consider what that amount needs to be and how you use it.

Adding to Your Future Income

Along with your future income, you may want to create additional currency for yourself following your post-work years to enhance your net worth further.

Think about the things you feel passionate about. Maybe you've wanted to write a book or enjoy making candles. Whatever your passion may be, you can often turn it into a way to bring in additional revenue, even by doing something you love just a few hours a week.

Your lifestyle activities do not all have to be non-income-producing **(NIP)** activities. Following your passion is not only fulfilling but can also lead you to great ways to continue earning income.

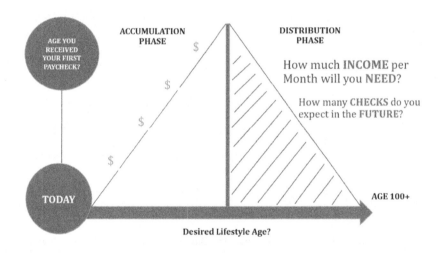

Risk Assessment

Yet another important consideration for your future is how much risk you will take to produce income. Some investments are riskier than others. As you age, they should get less risky. For many, that means shifting investments from those that fluctuate, like the stock market, to more stable investments, whether in real estate or annuities.

Distributing Your Money: The Rule of 25

One way to look at your finances as you age is by following **The Rule of 25.** This rule refers to spending your future retirement years living off a 4 percent withdrawal rate from your accumulated funds. The 4 percent Retirement Rule is also called the Safe Withdrawal rate. It suggests that without significantly depleting your nest egg, you can withdraw 4 percent of your savings annually for 30 years, adjusted for inflation.

Here is how it works following those guidelines. You start by withdrawing 4 percent of your retirement portfolio during your first post-work year. During the years that follow, your withdrawal amount is adjusted for inflation to ensure the stability of your purchasing power.

Whether this approach is successful depends on your maintaining a balanced portfolio of investments capable of generating the returns necessary to cover your yearly withdrawals and inflationary adjustments. It also depends on a typical retirement period of 30 years.

Mark and Veronica worked hard preparing for their retirement. Their financial advisor explained the 4 percent rule to them. The explanation was based on accumulated $1 million, allowing them to withdraw $40,000 their first year in retirement, with subsequent year withdrawal rates accounting for inflation. For example, if inflation were at 2 percent the following year, they could withdraw $40,800 in that second year.

The Rule of 25 and its 4 percent withdrawal rate serve as a guideline rather than a guarantee. Unexpected expenses and fluctuating market conditions could change things, making flexibility and regular reassessment key to the success of such a plan.

The reason for the figure of 4 percent is that if you try to take a larger percentage of your nest egg every year, say 5 percent or 6 percent, based on 30 retirement years, you could run the risk of running out of money during the years you're no longer working.

Maintaining and Envisioning Your Future Lifestyle

But it is important to look beyond the Rule of 25 and consider potential problems with this plan.

First, some of you may not have built up as much as a million dollars when saving for your future.

Second, even if you have accumulated a million dollars for your retirement years, that 4 percent withdrawal rate is unlikely to provide you with the same lifestyle you were living

THE 8 FINANCIAL BREAKTHROUGHS

when you were earning your income. Whether making $90,000 or $200,000 a year, reducing your income to that $40,000 withdrawal rate annually will lead to a definite reduction in your lifestyle. Is that something you accept, or do you want more to achieve your plans?

To answer that question, you must *envision the lifestyle you want* and figure out how to build it into your future.

Envision the big picture:

- What will you be doing when you are no longer working full time?
- How much money will you have?
- What will be the first thing you do when you wake up?
- What is important to you?

For most of us, achieving the lifestyle we desire requires treating ourselves as if we were a business.

Be entrepreneurial, save money, and build a business of one sort or another.

Assess Your Future with a Financial Professional

Most people never take the time to consider what they want their future lifestyles to look like, much less plan for it.

FPN INNOVATION TEAM

But wouldn't you want that business to succeed if you were your business?

One part of achieving that success is getting the input of a financial professional to assess your future and envision your lifestyle.

You owe it to yourself--and your future self--to spend at least an hour speaking with a financial professional about what is important to you to pursue.

To shape your future income and lifestyle, you need to start planning today.

"There is no passion to be found playing small—in settling for a life that is less than the one you are capable of living."

Nelson Mandela

THE 8 FINANCIAL BREAKTHROUGHS

Homework

- How do you see your future lifestyle unfolding?
- What is your passion in life?
- How much risk do you feel comfortable taking when investing in your future?
- Will the Rule of 25 work for you?
- What can you do to increase your lifestyle beyond the withdrawals that work well for the Rule of 25?
- Can you create income by following passion projects instead of relying on savings?
- Have you assessed how much you have saved for your future or considered the optimal savings amount for you?
- Schedule a time with a financial professional.

FPN INNOVATION TEAM

"Your net worth can fluctuate, but your self-worth should only appreciate."

Chris Gardner

Chapter 8

Building Your Net Worth

(Breakthrough # 6)

Once you start thinking about saving for your future life, you can highly likely see why you should build your net worth before you reach your golden years. Most people do not think about their net worth that often, even though building your net worth means building wealth.

If you do not build wealth, you may not have enough money to achieve your life goals.

I encourage my clients to think about what keeps them awake at night. Often, what keeps them up involves a fear of running out of money. That ties in with other worries, such as not living up to their potential, being a burden to their children or others, running out of time, or feeling like they do not deserve to "have it all."

So much of what I hear about frustrations and desires is focused on hoping that one will have enough money to survive.

But I want you to go beyond that. I want you to have the successful lifestyle you desire, an enduring legacy, and peace of mind.

Live the way you want to live, not the way you're forced to live once you're no longer working.

Bear in mind that there is no way to *save* yourself for retirement. Instead, you need to *build* your net worth to achieve your goals.

So, how can you build your net worth? To do so, you need to implement these four fundamental elements to set yourself up for better and more consistent income and net worth in retirement. The first step is to develop a solid budget. This will help you track your income and expenses, identify areas where you can cut back, and allocate funds towards savings and investments. Next, you will want to focus on increasing your income through career advancement, business, or investments.

THE 8 FINANCIAL BREAKTHROUGHS

These elements are:

- **Time**--Stay aware of your timeline for accumulating and distributing your income. Make sure you know how much time you have and how much time you need to reach your goals.
- **Money**--Save consistently every month. It does not matter how much you are saving. Just make sure you save it every month.
- **Rate of Return on Investments (ROI)**--You need to find investments that offer a consistent rate of return.
- **Tax Advantage Plan**--Establish a plan that fits your needs.

Along with implementing these four elements, you also need to:

- Establish consistent income.
- Own a home.
- Prepare for the possibility of the unexpected.

Preparing for the Unexpected

Preparing for the unexpected is essential. June and Chris did everything right to pursue the American Dream. They worked hard, paid their bills on time, and saved money in solid, traditional accounts. They felt that they had established a reasonable net worth and had planned for the future lifestyle they desired.

But one day, an emergency occurred. Their son was in a car accident. His bills went far beyond what both their medical and accident insurance covered, and to get him the help that he needed, from surgery to physical therapy, June and Chris wiped out their savings. That was it; they were back to zero and had to start saving again.

They were not prepared for this emergency. Their savings were set aside for their lifestyle retirement plan, and that was it. They did not build a large enough cash flow to establish an emergency fund separate from their lifestyle account. Neither they nor their son had purchased the life or disability insurance that could have been used to finance his care.

Unfortunately, Chris and June learned that emergencies could occur and derail everything without the appropriate savings and support plans.

On the other hand, Belinda put much thought into managing her future income. She had various buckets of money, including an opportunity fund, an emergency fund, and a lifestyle fund. Using her opportunity fund, she found and acted on new investment opportunities over time, building her net worth. Some risks were taken, but she was consistent with her savings and managing those different money buckets.

THE 8 FINANCIAL BREAKTHROUGHS

When an emergency arose, she had the life and disability insurance coverage she needed, and the savings earmarked for emergencies to take care of things.

Thus prepared, she stuck to her plans. Today, she has a better lifestyle than she did during her working years, which is the best end goal to achieve.

Today's Decisions Will Build Your Future Net Worth

People do not think about their net worth often enough. But you need to remember that your decisions today will build your future net worth and establish your future income or take it away.

Having a successful plan to fund your future lifestyle is the place to start. That plan should reflect the lifestyle you want.

To live the way you want, you need the wisdom to examine your income sources for retirement. Consider how much income you will need every month. As you save for the future, break down your financial journey.

For example, if you are getting a paycheck every week, will that paycheck be the same amount every week until you retire? If you believe that is the case, you need to determine whether your paycheck can handle the future lifestyle you desire and your lifestyle today.

People are living longer than ever before. Hallmark Cards recently conducted a research study and found there are more cards sold today wishing people a happy 90th and 100th birthday than at any other time in history.

When you combine the amount you are earning and saving with your potential for longevity, you must ensure you won't lose or run out of money. You need to know how to make more money.

If all your buckets of money are assigned a job, then make sure they are doing that job. Remember, you want a bucket for emergencies and one for opportunities, the kinds of financial opportunities that increase your net worth. You also want a bucket devoted to accumulating savings toward your future lifestyle.

Equally important: along with establishing a money bucket for emergencies, pay for the additional support you need to cover them.

Identifying Major Threats to Your Future

Four major threats can significantly affect your net worth, financial future, and legacy.

THE 8 FINANCIAL BREAKTHROUGHS

Disability and Major Health Concerns

As I've discussed earlier, one of the best ways to protect yourself against disability and major health concerns is through insurance. Along with protecting you from these threats, insurance is critical when you are looking toward providing a legacy.

Having disability and long-term care insurance will protect you by providing the necessary income should you experience a disability or a significant illness, such as cancer, a stroke, or a heart attack. It can also provide payment for long-term care should you become disabled or seriously ill.

Life insurance is also essential to add to your portfolio of protection. This kind of insurance can provide for your legacy.

Taxes

Unlike illness or injury, the threat of taxes can't be mitigated with the correct information. Instead, this threat can be dealt with by using financial wisdom to establish the best tax plan for you. This could mean acquiring tax-free investment options. It could mean moving your money from one form of retirement savings account, such as an IRA, to another, such as a Roth account. It could also involve handling your tax return, such as deferring a loss until it is needed to offset a gain.

Procrastination

Only you can successfully end the threat of procrastination. Act today to ensure the lifestyle you want and deserve in the future. Don't just think about establishing a plan for your future; do it!

Additional Threats

Of course, there are other threats to be aware of. These include identity theft or being waylaid by the wrong information. Monitoring your credit accounts and being careful not to provide personal information to people or websites you don't know can help prevent identity theft. When it comes to receiving or acting upon financial information, you should only rely on information obtained from a trusted financial professional or an established trusted financial publication.

Acquire Income Wisdom

Along the way, you need to gain income wisdom to establish the best uses for those separate buckets of money you're creating and how they will support your future.

You need to consider the necessities you need, your **M.U.G.**, and your **G.R.I.P.**

THE 8 FINANCIAL BREAKTHROUGHS

Consistency is always the key. Once you've established your timeline for achieving your financial needs and a consistent savings pattern, you need to find investments with a consistent and good rate of return over time. Utilize a good tax advantage plan so you're not returning your investments to the government when you retire. Each of these elements is part of income wisdom.

Remember, while having a home is essential, you can't remove a door from its hinges or a window from its sill and take those to the bank. You can't exchange those individual parts of your house for cash.

Many people feel that having a home is living the American dream. While that is partly true, having a consistent future income is equally vital to achieving that dream.

While the actual statistics and financial figures will vary, most Americans have only set aside $5,000 to fund their future. That's an incredibly small amount—far too small.

Invest more in yourself, opportunities and protection plan(s) to help you grow your net worth. That's income wisdom.

"We're trying to make money, trying to add a zero onto our net worth."

J. B. Pritzker

Homework

- What keeps you awake at night worrying about your future?
- Do you have disability, long-term care, and life insurance? Why or why not?
- Are you aware of your timeline heading toward retirement, and are you taking consistent actions to save for it and find the opportunities with the best rate of return?
- Have you acquired the financial wisdom to choose the right investments and tax adjustment plan?
- What is the way that you want to live after you stop working? What does that lifestyle look like to you?

THE 8 FINANCIAL BREAKTHROUGHS

"To double your net worth, double your self-worth. Because you will never exceed the height of your self-image."

Robin S. Sharma

Chapter 9

Improving Your Conversations About Net Worth

We have talked a lot about net worth, so let's consider your net worth: *the value of a person or corporation's assets minus the liabilities.* Of course, you need to determine your assets and liabilities and the best way to grow your assets.

You also need to guard against the threats that can arise and negatively affect your net worth.

Along with mitigating threats to your net worth, you must also ensure your future wealth by increasing it. If you do not focus on growing your wealth, your net worth is also at

THE 8 FINANCIAL BREAKTHROUGHS

risk. Growing your net worth is like a game of increase, a competition with yourself to accumulate more assets.

The Five Es of Change: Improving Your Financial Conversations

An essential part of playing the game of accumulation is changing the conversations you have about accumulating wealth. Employing what I call the five Es can change those conversations and change your life.

1. **Environment (Influence)**
   You need to elevate your environment and its influence on you. When you change your environment, your conversations will change. They are not about merely scraping by or being broke but establishing and gaining a net worth.

2. **Expectation**
   Once you have elevated your environment, expectations for your future will come into place.

3. **Execution (Action)**
   Those expectations will lead to acting on or executing them.

4. **Experience**

   Once you have acted on your expectations, you'll gain experience, which you can share with others and use to grow yourself.

5. **Example**

   By sharing your experience, you will be able to provide examples and hear and learn from others' examples.

Think of these Five Es in this way: you are invited to a large financial dinner with various tables, and everyone has a different financial conversation. Do you want to sit with the guests talking about being almost out of money or at the table where people discuss their opportunities and examples of how they improved their net worth?

Your income may very well be correlated to the income of the people you spend the most time with--that is your environment. A discussion by people who cannot afford their student loans differs from those who discuss investments and opportunities.

The words you use and the conversations you have will determine the kind of network you have available. Your network refers to the people you can discuss finances with, the people who can discuss and assist with the growth of your net worth.

THE 8 FINANCIAL BREAKTHROUGHS

Do you want Income Wisdom or Financial Advice?
Income wisdom means establishing consistent daily habits to contribute to your monthly savings so you can have consistency during your retirement! Time to have a seat at the table of wisdom.

Most people move from table to table at that financial dinner party throughout their lives.

Here is the order of money conversation that may be at different tables:

- Poor
- Broke
- Almost Making It
- Making it
- Just Getting By
- Getting By
- Savings/Giving
- Investing
- Net Worth
- Legacy/Inheritance
- Profit Margins
- Family Office

FPN INNOVATION TEAM

Most people start at a broken table conversation and then move up the ladder.

There are several of those conversations:

- Being broke and accepting it.
- Being broke and not knowing it--this is a scary table to sit at.
- Being broke, knowing it, but taking no action to change things.
- Being broke but determined to change that situation.

Once you reach that last broken table conversation, you graduate to the almost-making-it table, where your expectations start to take shape. Then, you join the next table by saving and beginning to invest. It's at that table when you start to execute your plans.

Once you've had experience in execution, you move to the net worth table. From there, you move to the table that discusses the most advantageous profit margins and finally to a table that discusses legacy and inheritance.

Everything comes down to having these different conversations and establishing different relationships because these conversations and relationships lead to connections. Your connections can elevate your net worth and change the table at which you're sitting.

THE 8 FINANCIAL BREAKTHROUGHS

Think of the relationships you are establishing as magnets that pull you toward the connections you need to establish for a successful future lifestyle.

"Your network is your net worth. How do you value your network? Well, if you don't value it, cultivate it, nurture it, it becomes worthless. If you do value it, it becomes priceless."

Robert G. Allen

Homework

- What kinds of conversations are you having about money?
- What financial "table" would you like to sit at, and how can you find your seat?
- Who can help you get to a new table?
- Schedule a time with a financial professional.

THE 8 FINANCIAL BREAKTHROUGHS

Unlock the secrets to transforming your financial life with our exclusive "The 8 Financial Breakthroughs" guide! Whether you want to enhance your savings, secure lifelong income, or optimize your tax strategies, this guide is your first step toward a prosperous future.

Do not miss out on these critical insights that could reshape your financial landscape. **Act now—Schedule a time with a financial professional to receive a complimentary Financial Discovery** Your breakthrough awaits, and the power to change your future is just one conversation away!

FPN INNOVATION TEAM

"Planning is bringing the future into the present."

Mike Vance

Chapter 10

Your Legacy

Preparing for the Future
(Breakthrough # 7)

We have discussed protecting ourselves against financial threats and improving our environment, expectations, actions, and experience.

Let us look beyond that at your legacy and succession plans.

Legacy and Succession

What does leaving a legacy mean to you? Does it mean passing along your grandmother's recipe for sweet potato pie or your uncle's BBQ sauce recipe? Does it mean passing on the family photo album full of old photos?

Is your legacy about passing on your family business, whether anyone in your family has decided they want to be a part of it or not? Perhaps you have one child who wants to run your business but two others who don't. How will you divide other assets equitably, such as your house or your grandmother's vacation cabin?

Whatever your decisions about legacy, documents are needed that clearly reveal who will get what asset and how your legacy will be divided.

Proper documentation is always necessary. This kind of documentation must be legal, not consist of your thoughts written on a napkin and tucked away in a drawer.

There are so many terrible stories about family disasters that could have easily been avoided with simple advance legacy planning.

Six Necessary Legal Documents

You should effectively use and file six necessary legal documents to avoid unfortunate family fights and discord.

Proper documentation ensures that your heirs will have the correct instructions regarding the distribution of your assets, such as receiving them upon their marriages or college graduation.

THE 8 FINANCIAL BREAKTHROUGHS

While we cannot control the narrative of our heirs' lives from beyond the grave, we can control their net worth by using proper documentation and filing those documents.

These documents include:

Will--Identifies the guardian of minor or special needs children or grandchildren. It spells out in writing who will carry out your wishes and how your property will be allocated and distributed.

Financial Power of Attorney--This document identifies who will control your affairs if you cannot. This could include handling bills, insurance payments, taxes, or maintaining and selling property.

Advance Health Care Directive or Living Will--A living will is designed to identify the person who can make health-care decisions for you if you cannot make them. This could include handling bills, insurance payments, taxes, or maintaining and selling property.

Health Insurance Portability and Accountability Act (HIPPA)--This document allows the person serving as your health-care agent to have access to your medical records and insurance information. Access to information can assist in your treatment when you are unable to do so.

Life Insurance Trust--Establishing a life insurance trust is essential to support your legacy. Such a trust minimizes estate taxes and simplifies access to funds for your inheritors. For example, it is much easier to distribute cash from a life insurance trust than from selling antiques, jewelry, and collectibles. A life insurance trust does not need to pass through probate.

Revocable and Irrevocable Trusts--Along with a life insurance trust, there are two common types of trusts to protect your personal and/or business assets: revocable and irrevocable trusts.

The difference between the two is simple. **Revocable Trusts** are easier to set up, and if changes are necessary, they are easy to modify. On the other hand, irrevocable trusts cannot be changed after they are created, at least not without considerable difficulty.

Irrevocable Trusts have important estate tax benefits. Revocable trusts do not provide these benefits.

An irrevocable trust also keeps your assets out of the reach of creditors, a divorced spouse, business partners, or anyone else who might seek access to your assets. But along with being essentially set in stone, an irrevocable trust means that you'll cede more control of your finances, and additional tax returns may be necessary.

The main thing to remember about trusts is that they should be protective. Information in the trust will protect what you have indicated as your wishes in a will.

What Is Your Desired Outcome?

A personal exit strategy is crucial to achieving the desired outcome for your financial legacy. No one will be here forever; therefore, having a trust allows you to plan a future you would like your heirs to enjoy.

Like any other part of your finances, estate planning is necessary to preserve your legacy for future generations.

"Before anything else, preparation is the key to success."

Alexander Graham Bell

Homework

- Have you set up a will or other documents to protect your legacy? Why or why not?
- Are you aware of the differences between a revocable and irrevocable trust? Which type of trust might work better for you?
- Have you spent the necessary time to plan your estate?
- Have you spoken to a legal or other representative to administer a trust?
- Do you have an estate attorney?

THE 8 FINANCIAL BREAKTHROUGHS

"Legacy is not what I did for myself. It's what I'm doing for the next generation."

Vitor Belfort

Chapter 11

Establishing Your Business Legacy
(Breakthrough # 7)

Establishing your legacy is a critical area of future planning. If you own a business or are a partner, establishing your business succession and legacy is also necessary.

Shaping Your Business Exit Strategy
(The Cathy Family)

Essentially, you need to put the same level of planning and care into a strategy for successfully exiting your business as you do in planning your legacy.

THE 8 FINANCIAL BREAKTHROUGHS

There are always so many questions to answer regarding a business sale. You do not want a legacy to be handled chaotically, or customer service, product quality, and the business itself could suffer. The success of the company would falter.

The successful Chick-fil-A fast food chain worked hard to ensure a seamless transition between generations. When CEO Truett Cathy stepped down, the chain was moving into its fourth generation of family ownership.

For many businesses, the odds are low that a family-owned business will survive past the third generation. Some of this is because of a lack of cooperation among family members, communication, or interest.

The best way to prevent business failings is to communicate well and use early succession planning between each generation. It helps to think of succession as a long, ongoing transition rather than a single occurrence or event.

One way to ensure communication is to establish succession documents that include requirements for more than just annual meetings between company stakeholders. Setting up regular meetings allows the time to review successes and failures, relationships, and the dynamics among family members over time.

Using the Cathy family as an example, their succession plans also required family members to graduate from college and work outside the family business for at least two years before working for Chick-fil-A. Family members must also go through the same employment process as other applicants. The company's succession documents also have a wealth transfer program in place.

Other techniques the company uses include establishing an advisory board that requires a regular review of policies, financial statements, and upcoming succession plans and setting up required meetings.

Finally, the business has passed on more than just the financial aspects of its heritage. The Cathy family has also successfully passed along the company's original customer service culture.

Preserving Your Legacy for Generations
(The Carter Family)

The Carter family lived in and operated their thriving family business in a small town. They were well-known for their successful business and for establishing a firmly rooted commitment to preserving their legacy. They wanted to ensure that it was preserved for future generations.

Family patriarch Thomas Carter was well-informed about succession planning and its importance in building a lasting family legacy.

When he got older, he called a meeting with his family to share his wisdom and vision. During the meeting, he sincerely expressed his belief that the business, a cornerstone of the family for many years, should continue. He noted that the business was not just about the past, what had been built, or the family's success. He told them that establishing a legacy was all about ensuring the endurance of the business even after he and his children and grandchildren were gone.

His family listened and carefully considered his desire to create a solid succession plan that would identify future family leaders and successfully equip them with the knowledge and skills necessary to continue the family's legacy over the years to come.

Thomas presented a comprehensive plan. He outlined a plan emphasizing the importance of collaboration and innovation, a culture where every family member would have their talents valued and recognized. He explained that the family legacy plan should include everything from mentoring programs to leadership development and outline a clear path to advancement within the company.

Of course, beyond establishing a legacy of business success, Thomas knew the family legacy should include carrying forward shared values and traditions. This family culture would be the glue that would hold the family together through multiple generations.

He reminded his family not to forget their roots. He stressed that their true legacy was built on "integrity, hard work, and compassion." He asserted that those values should guide everything the family did in the future in their personal lives and business ventures.

The words of their patriarch inspired the other members of the Carter family, and they began to establish a succession and family legacy plan along Thomas's lines. Their plan focused on honoring their past, empowering their present, and presenting the goals, wisdom, and purpose that would continue to inspire their future.

The family set up regular meetings to discuss important decisions to achieve their plan. They celebrated personal business milestones together. The family also began documenting their family history for future generations, thus preserving stories and memories.

Along with a legacy plan for the business itself, the family examined both estate planning and wealth transfer strategies. By addressing these areas of legacy, they could ensure their assets would be equitably and smoothly distributed to future generations.

As important as each aspect of establishing their legacy was, Thomas set the family on an even more important path: making time for each other and nurturing their family bonds, which went far beyond preserving their business and wealth.

The Carters cherished spending time together, sharing meals, taking family vacations, and even coming together to enjoy family game nights. Thomas had galvanized them to understand that their family bond was their legacy's truest and most valuable part.

With this bond firmly in place, the Carter family continued to thrive, and their legacy flourished. New business leaders were well-guided by the values and principles their predecessors practiced; the family continued to be united, and their legacy endured as a powerful testament to their unity, love, and shared sense of purpose.

Components of Succession and Legacy Planning

Remember, when you build a succession and legacy plan for your family business, it should always serve to establish a heritage for future generations. It should preserve family values and wealth.

The components that go into succession and legacy planning should include each of the following areas:

Define Your Objectives

The place to start is by identifying and clarifying your goals and objectives. What do you want your succession and legacy plan to achieve? Which of these areas of legacy are your main purpose?

- Ensuring the continued success of the family business
- Preserving family wealth
- Passing down values and traditions
- A combination of each of the above

Identify Successors

Once you have defined your objectives, it's time to evaluate potential successors' skills, experience, and commitment. Identify those who exhibit leadership qualities, business knowledge and skill, and alignment with family values and vision when determining who is most committed to leading the business into the future.

Develop Leadership and Management Skills

Along with identifying potential successors and providing the training, mentorship, and opportunities for development, these individuals would need to assume leadership roles within the family business.

This development could include:

- On-the-job training.
- Formal education.
- Participation in industry associations.

THE 8 FINANCIAL BREAKTHROUGHS

- Exposure to different areas of the business.

Establish Structures for Governance

You should also define clear and concise structures for governance and decision-making. These structures should guide the succession process, ensuring transparency, fairness, and accountability. These structures could include the creation of a board of directors or the establishment of a family council. These bodies would oversee key decisions related to both business and family affairs.

Address Ownership and Equity Transfer

Determining how ownership and equity will be transferred to the next generation is also essential.

You will need to consider:

- Tax implications.
- Estate planning considerations.
- Financial needs of both the business and individual family members.

You may need to utilize buy-sell agreements, trusts, or other legal tools for estate planning.

Document Policies and Procedures

Another essential aspect of legacy planning is clearly defining and documenting the business's policies, procedures, and best practices. You should focus on these areas related to succession planning, governance, and family communication. Doing so will assist you in achieving continuity for the business and provide a framework of knowledge for future generations.

Communicate Openly and Transparently

It is also essential to foster open, transparent communication regarding your succession and legacy plan. This communication should include family members, stakeholders, and key employees. To build consensus and align the company's values you should encourage dialogue, address any concerns, and solicit input from all parties.

Preserve Family Values and Traditions

Preserving family values and traditions is crucial to any legacy. Identify your most integral core values, beliefs, and traditions. Once you have done so, integrate them into the succession and legacy plan.

THE 8 FINANCIAL BREAKTHROUGHS

This integration can be accomplished by:

- Creating a family mission statement.
- Holding family retreats or reunions.
- Documenting family history and stories.

Plan for Continuity and Contingencies

You will also want to consider potential challenges and disruptions to your succession and legacy plan. Disruptions could include unexpected events, illnesses or disabilities, conflicts, or changes in the overall business environment. To ensure business continuity and resilience, develop contingency plans and the mechanisms necessary to accomplish them.

Regularly Review and Update Your Succession and Legacy Plan

It is also important to monitor and evaluate the effectiveness of your succession and legacy plan over time. Make any necessary adjustments based on changes in circumstances, evolving goals, or lessons learned from experience.

When you are proactive and follow these steps for succession and legacy planning, you ensure that your family can enjoy continued business success and prosperity and preserve your family heritage.

Start with the Succession Basics

On a more basic level, you need to determine whether your children or other relatives want to take on your business or whether you would be better served by selling it and distributing the proceeds.

Sometimes, determining a business interest and making plans to serve the needs of every family member can require difficult conversations, but they are necessary, nonetheless.

Find out what those near and dear to you genuinely want to do rather than taking it for granted that they will join the family business and be your successors.

Remember, when it comes to your company's culture, if you have important traits that you want to pass on or areas that you want to ensure your business continues to represent, this should be discussed and formalized as well.

You don't just pass down assets--you pass down behaviors in a solid succession plan.

These behaviors include moral and legal choices, risk-taking behavior, and every aspect of your business integrity.

THE 8 FINANCIAL BREAKTHROUGHS

Continuing to Work for Your Company After Exiting

In some cases, establishing a transition plan for your business may include keeping your hand on the wheel at least a little longer after you choose to exit.

Perhaps you'll stay on as a majority shareholder with decision-making capabilities or as a consultant. Or perhaps you'll choose to continue working at your company without having to handle the executive decisions.

Working as a consultant or stepping down from your role as CEO and continuing to be a part of your company in whatever way suits you best still allows you to do what you love but eliminates the responsibility that goes with it. At the same time, you get to shepherd your company through the transition and guide the new owners in their success story, whether they are family owners or not.

The Essentials of Business Legacy and Succession

In summary, the essentials involved in building a legacy and succession plan for your business include passing on behaviors to assure future success, establishing financial structure, and deciding what continued role you would like to play, if any, when you step away from your role as leader.

FPN INNOVATION TEAM

In short, you are not only considering money when you set up a business succession plan. You're talking about future decision-making and the best ways to guide and handle your business transition--your company and yourself.

"It is up to us to live up to the legacy that was left for us, and to leave a legacy that is worthy of our children and of future generations."

Christine Gregoire

THE 8 FINANCIAL BREAKTHROUGHS

Homework

- Have you discussed the future of your business legacy with your family?
- Do you have a plan in place for who will run the business after you make your exit? Why or why not?
- How do you see your role in the business after you step down from a leadership role?
- Do you want to continue to work in the business after you leave your current position?
- What behaviors or policies would you want to pass on as a business legacy?
- When was the last time you had a business valuation done?
- What is the value of your business?

FPN INNOVATION TEAM

"Accountability breeds response-ability."

Stephen R. Covey

Chapter 12

Accountability
(Breakthrough # 8)

What does it mean to be accountable? You may notice that accountability is made up of two words: count and ability. The word speaks to the idea of being able to count on your ability to make lifestyle decisions, create present and future income, and establish a legacy.

Everything has a number, from your driver's license to the weight on your scale and the speed limit sign to your phone number. You are accountable to those numbers, and you accept them. We live in a world of numbers.

But when it comes to money, sometimes we fight to be accountable for those numbers. That does not mean being accountable for money isn't important--quite the opposite. You are accountable to your family, earning income, and future.

You are accountable for your legacy, lifestyle decisions, and net worth growth.

But because it is human nature to avoid this kind of accountability, having a third-party financial professional can be key to your success.

Working with a Financial Professional

A financial professional can hold you accountable without emotion or personal feelings affecting them. For this reason, it is not a good idea to have a close friend or family member serve as your financial accountability partner. Emotions always come into play.

On the other hand, who or what cannot hold you accountable but help you recognize your responsibilities and coach you through the best ways to achieve them?

Accountability and responsibility are different. Responsibility means knowing what to do, while accountability means someone is helping you see what you did or did not do.

Let's say you want to lose ten pounds and know you need to workout every day. You and you alone are responsible for achieving this, but your gym trainer will hold you accountable, tell you when to come in, and coach you through the most efficient exercises.

You will not want to let your coach down, so you do your push-ups and pull-ups. Without that coach, would you really go to the gym at 6 a.m. every day and run through that exercise routine? Probably not. But your coach's presence holds you accountable.

A professional helps you look at things through a different, detached lens. If your spouse holds you accountable, emotion could be the only thing you listen to. Your loved one could also be trying to pacify your feelings rather than hold you accountable for a logical decision.

That does not mean you shouldn't have someone close to you holding you accountable; it just means you need an unbiased eye to guide you.

The Positive and Negative Sides of Accountability

There are positive and negative sides to being accountable--reward and punishment.

As a child, you clean your room and put away your toys because your parents tell you that is your responsibility. But you also do it because they will hold you accountable if you do not.

FPN INNOVATION TEAM

Maybe being accountable means getting a reward for dessert, such as ice cream. You will get punished if you're not accountable and won't get any ice cream.

You must go to the principal's office if you are in school and receive detention. That idea scares you, so you stay accountable and do your homework because you're worried about that punishment.

When you go to college, reward and punishment become very clear. For example, if you must write a term paper, you must be accountable for completing it on time.

If you don't do so, you may fail the class. You're kicked out of college if you steal someone else's paper and cheat.

But, on the other hand, if you do your work on time and do an excellent job, you will make it onto the Dean's List. That's the punishment and the reward side of accountability. As you age, you will likely be the only one holding yourself accountable.

Unless you're a die-hard do-it-yourself, you will often hire others to be accountable for your responsibilities. For example, if your roof needs repair, you hire a roofer to fix it rather than getting on a ladder yourself. If you need a knee replacement, a surgeon must perform the surgery. These are examples of things we immediately know we cannot possibly be accountable for.

But when it comes to money, things can be extremely sensitive. After all, if we earn income every week, we don't

THE 8 FINANCIAL BREAKTHROUGHS

feel like we need someone to hold us accountable. We think we are doing it all.

Money can create real accountability issues. There are many stories about lottery winners or famous individuals who have gone broke because they were not accountable, and the people who had coached them were not accountable either.

Many people simply can't make decisions on their own and need a sounding board. If you are driving your car and accidentally drift out of your lane, you may need to hear someone blow their horn to remind you to get back in the lane.

The same is true of money management. We all get off track sometimes and need someone to remind us to get back on it.

While it is important and supportive to consult with your spouse or your significant other about money, particularly when it comes to enormous amounts, you need an impartial, outside source to hold you accountable.

Select Your Coach

When choosing an outside accountability coach, you want someone you can trust to review your goals and actions. You also need to share the same values.

FPN INNOVATION TEAM

We ask our clients ten questions to ensure we are on the same page and that my team and I coach you as financial professionals.

Some of the questions we ask include what motivated them to meet with us, what they hope to accomplish, what their biggest challenge is, and how long it has been on their minds. We also ask about their financial goals—what is their most important goal, and are they currently earning enough to support their goals and dreams?

We try to get to the heart of what they value and believe and the ways they can achieve their goals. Along with sharing the same values and philosophies, I believe you should be a good listener and be accountable.

When you appoint someone to help you, you give them a high level of accountability. That person is both responsible and accountable to you.

You need someone to help you move between the various levels of wealth:

- Financial **Stability**
- Financial **Security**
- Financial **Freedom**
- Financial **Abundance**

If you're not being held accountable, you can all too easily go down the old path you have always followed. What is that path? Well, for many people, their path leads only as far as financial security and stops right there.

The problem is that, along with that security, you may be stuck at a job you do not like without the time to do the things you love. You are going through the motions and thinking, "I should've. I could've."

An accountable financial professional can stop you from going through life's motions. They can redirect you so you can find new and greater cash flow, spend more time with your family, and enjoy your life more.

That is important in appointing the right financial professional. They should keep you from straying from your goals, encourage you to move forward and prevent you from stopping short of your potential.

Without that kind of accountability and guidance, it is far too easy to become attracted to the next rip-off or get-rich scheme. My job is to prevent people from doing something crazy with their money and encourage them to listen to their gut feelings, behave logically, and stick to a financial plan.

Lionel's Story

Lionel's story is a cautionary tale. He retired from law enforcement with over seven figures in his bank account. He was happy to be retired. But, beyond that, he had no real plans.

Lionel began loaning his money to family members for various international business ventures. He did not question any of them about the deals; they were all putting the money into the same collective venture.

Unfortunately, that venture did not work out, and they all lost the money Lionel had given them. On top of that, no one had enough money to pay him back.

So, Lionel lost his retirement money, and his family never paid him back. To this day, there is much friction between Lionel and his family.

Had Lionel appointed a financial professional to vet that deal and hold him accountable for formulating good retirement goals, the situation would not have happened. Instead, Lionel relied on what he thought sounded like a good opportunity based on what his family members told him.

Establishing Your Family Office

Once you reach an income status that has increased your net worth and taken you to a level of abundance, it's time to set up your family office.

Your family office gives you a new level of accountability.

THE 8 FINANCIAL BREAKTHROUGHS

You build a talented team when you set up your family office. You add new members to that team as you build your net worth. Each member shares their goals and philosophies but performs a different role. Like a quarterback, a running back, and a left tackle all perform different roles on a football team, the members of your family office follow the same accountability guidelines their coach gives them, but they each have their own function.

Your team members should include those involved in:

- Retirement planning
- Tax services.
- Trustee services
- Administrative services
- Accounts payable and receivable
- Cash management.
- Legal counsel
- Investment management
- Life Insurance manager
- Foundation management for philanthropy
- Real estate management
- Business management

Naturally, you will not fill out your team roster all at once. Rather, you will add your players as needed. You may start with a few people, say your accountant, attorney, or financial professional. Most people do not begin their family office until they have made a very substantial amount of money. However, starting small and building your team early is fine so you will be ready to expand.

You should always start with your financial professional or accountant because you will need the money to pay everyone.

You can build your family office from there. Building and having a team in your corner is always a good and supportive idea. Every winning team has an amazing coach who fills his roster with those who can help identify opportunities and hold you accountable.

Communication in the Family Office

Just as in any office organization, communication is vital. Perhaps that means weekly check-ins, once a quarter, or once a year. In my family office, we meet quarterly, with everyone present. This kind of regular contact and communication is why we work well together.

When you are ready to set up a family office, it depends on your net worth and income level. Your family

THE 8 FINANCIAL BREAKTHROUGHS

team members work only for you and do not work part-time or on an occasional basis.

You must establish a firm vision for your family office and avoid division. If you are not all on the same page, you can be flexible and change the players on your team.

As successes happen, make sure to thank all the members of your office. It is not just your success; it's "our success." Sometimes, positive changes and developments only come because we are being held accountable by the other team members.

After all, if you have a strong family office, you're building a firm foundation for your net worth and all your future business and philanthropic activities. You are moving toward your legacy. And there is always someone you can count on who will be checking for any blind spots or wrong turns.

"At the end of the day, we are accountable to ourselves. Our success is a result of what we do."

Catherine Pulsifer

Homework

- What does accountability mean to you?
- Have you experienced both positive and negative consequences of being held accountable?
- Have you appointed someone to hold you accountable for growing your wealth?
- What financial stage are you at today?
- Do you feel stuck at one level or another?
- What can you do to get unstuck? Do you have someone who can help you move forward?
- When you are ready to start your family office, do you have the people in your orbit who can help you maintain a strong, winning team?

THE 8 FINANCIAL BREAKTHROUGHS

"Money is usually attracted, not pursued."

Jim Rohn

Chapter 13

The Four Levels of Wealth

I have spoken briefly about the concept of
FOUR LEVELS OF WEALTH:

- Financial **Stability**
- Financial **Security**
- Financial **Freedom**
- Financial **Abundance**

Now, let us dive deeper and consider what each level may mean for you. Each is equally important for your financial well-being.

THE 8 FINANCIAL BREAKTHROUGHS

Financial Stability

Establishing financial stability is a huge step in many people's lives. When you reach a level of stability, you can pay your bills. Even if you have less than $200 left in your checking account at the end of the month, you are not worried. There will be more money coming in next month.

Financial Security

Financial security is a big step up from being stable. If you are secure, perhaps you have a year's worth of savings in the bank, no or very little credit card debt, and a promising job with no fear of layoffs.

You may also have enough connections in your industry that even if you did lose your job, you know you could find another. You have those savings to support you, in any case. You know you would be OK if something happened and one of your children needed medical care. Having at least a year in savings means feeling secure, even in an emergency or job loss.

Financial Freedom

When you reach financial freedom, you will not need to worry about money or think about it. You have enough money to make choices, even if that means taking a year-long vacation.

Financial freedom allows you to do what you want, when and with whom.

Financial freedom also offers you more time. You cannot enjoy the freedom of time without financial freedom. But even if you were given time and the ability to make choices, you still need to make responsible decisions. You can lose that freedom and find yourself back at the level of financial security without that freedom if you abuse it.

Financial Abundance

However, when you reach the level of financial abundance, you no longer have any risk of dropping a financial level. Once you reach the level of abundance, you have reached the financial stratosphere. It is the level at which, if some of your assets fall to the side, it will not affect you.

At this level, there is a different mindset. It is a mindset where you have amazing cash flow and never have to worry about money again.

THE 8 FINANCIAL BREAKTHROUGHS

Climbing the Money Conversation Ladder

Remember my description of a financial dinner party, where we move from table-to-table conversing about different financial topics? As we grow financially, the goal is to reach the table where the conversation is about abundance. That's the top of the money conversation ladder.

You start at one "broke" table, culminating with a move from the table at which you are broke but determined to change things.

The typical financial conversation moves from that fourth broke table to almost making it, to just getting by, to saving and giving. From that point, you graduate to investing, from investing to net worth, from a conversation about net worth to one about profit margins. Then, you move on to discussions about legacy and inheritance, with the last conversation being about the family office. Each is a different conversation, and only at the last table will you speak the language of abundance.

While you must start at one table, it is possible you may not start at the net worth table. The good news is that you know the money conversation at the table. Wherever you start, you are climbing *the money conversation ladder.*

These conversations lead to relationships and connections. Perhaps you can have a conversation in which you ask those at your table if they'd prefer to have an 800-

credit score or a half-million dollars. I prefer a half-million dollars because you can build your credit score after getting the money. Or maybe you can ask those at your table how they feel about their financial decisions or how much wealth they want to leave for the next generation. These questions fit different conversations on the money conversation ladder at different tables or rungs. Do not make statements. Ask questions and learn from the answers.

Your words locate your position anywhere in life. But does your financial profile match the profile you have on social media?

Money is a mindset. Having abundant money is a completely different mindset. Still, you must keep growing financially, moving up that conversational ladder. It can be difficult for people to move to a different, better table of financial conversation.

Making a Change

Making a change considers those five Es I spoke about earlier. Your environment and its influence are the first things you need to change to climb the money conversation ladder.

Once you change your environment, you change your narrative because you have moved to a different place. Then comes that second change: expectation. You will have higher

THE 8 FINANCIAL BREAKTHROUGHS

expectations in a new environment, and you need to meet those expectations.

Next, you need to execute or act on what you heard in your new environment. Acting is what is expected of you now. Once you do, you reach that fourth E: experience.

There you are, in a new environment with new expectations and new experiences on the actions you executed. At this point, you are the example that others will follow.

But if you never change your environment and influences, you will remain where you are and will not change.

Instead, you will be like a crab in the bucket. You will keep trying to impress others with no money that you're not broke. It is a toxic environment, and you're trapped in that bucket because you don't want to change. You have dug deep into that bucket and don't want to leave, even if people are cheering you on, telling you to come out. Many people decorate that bucket, making it the best one ever, but are still stuck in it because that is where they feel the most comfortable.

So, how do you climb out of that bucket? Even if you want to do so, it can be a challenge and feel awkward. In eighth grade, I was extremely gifted in math, but in all other subjects, I was just average. Because of my math skills, my school took me out of my regular classroom and put me in a new environment of very smart, gifted kids.

I went from being in the top 30 of my regular classes to being among the lowest in that new environment. That was a necessary challenge for me to grow. It was difficult for me, but I had to stick it out and work my way through it because, at first, it felt like the classroom was on a different level from me.

When you move into a new, better environment, it is natural to be excited and nervous because you may not feel like you fit in. Being around new people, you can learn from and grow with is exciting. Still, you feel nervous because you wonder if you even belong sharing that space, the same conversational table.

No Change, No Gain

In life, you need to move forward consistently. As you move forward, you will reach a fork in the road; when you reach that point, you must decide where you want to go.

Also, I had to decide which high school I would attend in eighth grade. I had to choose whether to go to the neighborhood school where my friends were going or to a rival school where I had more opportunities to pursue sports, music, and the arts. Later in life, I moved from my hometown, where the population was approximately 350,000 to Atlanta, a city of approximately 5,000,000 people. Later still, I decided to start my own firm.

THE 8 FINANCIAL BREAKTHROUGHS

These are the kinds of decisions that will shape your life. You'll feel uncomfortable at first, but you must keep moving forward.

You will have ups and downs; you'll experience setbacks and lessons. You will need to overcome periods of adversity. As you step forward into who you want to become, there is an element of sacrifice.

But I believe very strongly that *the pain you will feel remaining the same is much greater than the pain that comes with change.* It will certainly last longer. There may be more intensified pain when you push yourself to change, but it does not last forever.

Remember, being in the right environment is the key to building wealth. *Build your wealth, and everything will change in your life.* You must change your environment to start that forward movement. If you do not change your environment, you won't change your relationships or start new conversations.

You will not be introduced to those who will help you grow or form those new relationships. Getting that introduction is the most important thing of all. It is even more important than the conversations you'll have.

If the right person introduces you—someone credible who you like and trust—you will build relationships and conversations.

You may be introduced to new people or new ideas and new behaviors. You cannot receive those introductions unless you are willing to change your environment. One new conversation can lead to your next financial breakthrough. At the end of the day, all we have is our relationships and conversations.

Putting Yourself First

As businessman and author Robert Kiyosaki says,

> *"It's not how much money you make, but how much money you keep, how hard it works for you, and how many generations you keep it for."*

Most of us put ourselves last in our lives. Like any change, putting yourself first can be difficult. This is especially true when it comes to saving money.

We are so used to just paying our bills with one little click and putting ourselves and our needs last. But try to visualize the process in another way.

You come home from a hard day of work, and a line of people is waiting for you. They all want to get paid: the gas company, the electric company, the mortgage company, the credit card company. And they all start telling you how much you owe them. Visualizing that scene may make it clearer:

THE 8 FINANCIAL BREAKTHROUGHS

sometimes, you need to cut through that line and pay yourself first. Then pay the others. Then pay the others.

How much money can you save? Maybe it doesn't feel like much, but as I've said before, you must save every month no matter what. Write that number down. Share it with others or say the amount out loud. Remember that number, commit to it, and put yourself first.

As soon as you do that, ask yourself why you are saving that money and what its purpose is going to be. What is the job you are going to assign to that money? We also discussed this concept: every pile of money has its purpose.

Once you have determined the amount you are saving and what it will be used for, you'll feel more excited about saving and more committed to putting yourself first. This emotional connection to savings drives people to put themselves first.

Most people move not because they see the light but because they feel the heat.

Dr. Robert Anthony

So, your motivation for saving could be that you are not going to slip back to the financial table of broke people or that you're not going to work hard for any reason. Everyone will have a different answer, but locking into that emotional motivation to save is key.

FPN INNOVATION TEAM

Let us look at an example:

If I handed a sheet of paper to 100 people and asked them; when you hear the word money, what is the first word you think of? I would probably get 100 different answers. Some might say the money they are saving will pay off a student loan, while others may say they will use it to invest and make more money.

The bottom line is this: everyone needs money as a tool to create the lifestyle they desire. Do not put yourself last. Give your money purpose and create the tool you need for the lifestyle you want, your family, your future, and your legacy.

When you cut the line and put yourself first, then you can clearly see:
- How much money you can save?
- The reason you are saving the money.
- Where do you want to put that money?

Having a financial professional's wisdom guide you through how to use your money can help you create the right narrative for its use and develop the situational awareness you need to build wealth.

"A simple fact that is hard to learn is that the time to save money is when you have some."

Joe Moore

THE 8 FINANCIAL BREAKTHROUGHS

Homework

- What rung are you on in the conversational ladder of money? What can you do to move to the next rung?
- Commit to putting yourself first and start saving. What will you do with the money you have saved? What does accountability mean to you?
- Have you ever moved to a new situation where you felt uncomfortable?
- What did you do when it was time to move into a new situation?
- Did you recognize that the move was necessary, even painful? Why or why not?
- Are you ready to have a conversation with a financial professional?

FPN INNOVATION TEAM

"Change makes you find your calling, your legacy, and God's divine plan for your life. Don't run from it."

Iman

Chapter 14

The Legacy Ladder

Building your legacy and climbing the ladder to it starts with earning money. There are four ways to do this.

Employee

If you are an employee, you are working for other people, keeping hours that others set, and taking a lunch break. When you retire, you will get a watch and a cheap dinner at a chain restaurant. Of course, some people love their jobs, and naturally, businesses need employees to run successfully. But you will always be working for someone else.

Self-Employed

If you are self-employed, you provide a professional service to others in exchange for payment. Perhaps you're a lawyer, a real estate agent, or a salesperson. Regardless of your profession, you will not make any money if you decide to take a day off work. For some self-employed people, this may make less difference than for others.

Business Owner

As a business owner, you will potentially own a scalable, profitable system. However, some business owners will have profits, and some will not. The amount may vary. Some businesses will not be scalable because the business is based solely on the owner's talent or skill. To truly be a business owner, you need to have a profitable and scalable system. For more information, please refer to Robert Kiyosaki's book, "The Cashflow Quadrant."

Legacy Creator

If you are a legacy creator, you build generational wealth that will last at least a hundred years. Every decision you make now is building for the future. You have opened the door to freedom for yourself and future generations. You will

THE 8 FINANCIAL BREAKTHROUGHS

be leaping out of whatever little red box you have placed yourself in.

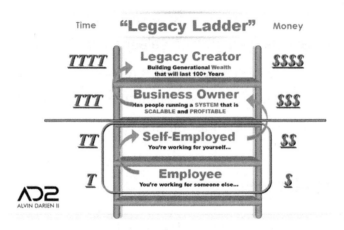

From Phone Sales to Creating Legacy

When I turned 24, I began building a business and becoming a legacy creator. At the time, I was working in a mall kiosk selling phones. I was self-employed, selling different brands of phone plans. It was simply about making money.

On the side, I helped clients with their finances. *That was always where my heart was, but I still felt like I had* to keep my job selling phones. One day, I had a real life-changing moment.

One of my financial clients was shopping in the mall, and she saw me working in that kiosk. She was shocked to see me. She could not believe that the same person who was successfully helping her grow her money was also selling phone plans at the mall.

I am sure it would be as if you had seen your doctor working at a Jiffy Lube, with grease under his fingernails. My client's shocked look made me feel uncomfortable. It was time for me to believe in my future fully. I resigned the next week.

That incident was one of my defining moments. I had to choose how I wanted my life to go. I wanted to be a legacy creator.

I had another defining moment when cancer hit me during my senior year in college. This situation taught me the powerful message of the importance of having financial protection against illness and disability. It also taught me a lesson that I really took to heart: how important it is to keep moving forward in life, to keep going and connecting with others, and to help others as well as yourself.

We do not know how long we have to live. Still, if we keep going and establish meaningful relationships, we will have much better and more positive lives.

Do You Want Freedom?

Part of being a legacy creator is achieving freedom. It is not just about financial freedom; it is also about time. Doctors make a lot of money but have little free time. If you are just looking for a job, you may have plenty of time but no money.

Being a legacy creator, you can achieve the freedom of financial success and still have freedom of time. As writer and publisher Margaret Bonnano says, "Being rich is having money; being wealthy is having time."

Some people have worked 40 hours a week for 40 years and only receive 40 percent of the income they deserve. However, there is another way. Remember, establishing a family office is your goal. Being a legacy creator is how you can accomplish just that.

You can follow the same old path you have always followed or the new one ahead of you.

THE OLD PATH LEADS TO:

- Being stuck in a job you hate.
- Lacking time to do the things that you love.
- Lacking financial abundance.
- Repeating your mistakes.
- Going through the motions in life instead of really living as you want.
- No Retirement
- Less Vacations

THE NEW PATH LEADS TO:

- Having more cash flow.
- Spending more time with your family.
- Enjoying more vacations.
- Getting paid what your worth.
- Controlling your future.
- Having a solid retirement plan.

Remember, there are financial threats you can avoid, and there are dreams you can turn into reality and achieve.

"Worry about going out there and making your own legacy."

Floyd Mayweather Jr.

Homework

- What drives you to succeed?
- How can you build a team to help you achieve your goals?
- Where are you on the legacy ladder? Where do you want to be?
- Have you experienced a defining moment in your life?
- What was that moment?
- How can you use that to build toward your legacy?

FPN INNOVATION TEAM

"Rich people believe 'I create my life.' Poor people believe 'Life happens to me.'"

T. Harv Eker

Conclusion

Are you ready to create your new life instead of letting life just happen? I hope that this book has helped you start on the path to shaping and creating the life you deserve.

Of course, just like me, you must commit to investing in yourself and your future. If you follow the eight financial breakthroughs we discussed, you can be assured of a positive financial present and future.

The 8 Financial Breakthroughs

These 8 steps allow you to take on your future, build your financial conversation, and become the legacy creator you deserve to be. Create your purpose, and you will achieve the freedom you want, financially and with your time.

Are you ready to transform your financial life? The 8 Financial Breakthroughs are your roadmap to financial security and freedom. Do not let another day go by without taking control of your future. Book your appointment today and discover the power of personalized financial guidance. Your financial breakthrough awaits!

Financial Education (1)

Your freedom starts with your financial education.

- Enhance it.
- Discover your financial DNA.
- Utilize the support of financial courses and seminars that can help you achieve financial wisdom.

Protection from Threats (2)

Protecting yourself from threats is essential for your future. **By implementing these strategies, you can protect yourself against threats to your income and create a secure financial future.**

- Protect yourself against income loss with the necessary insurance.
- Protect yourself from critical and chronic illness and disability with long-term care plans and life insurance.
- Protect yourself from inflation with investments that will cushion you from its impact.
- Protect yourself from running out of money with the investments that will allow you to achieve your financial goals.

THE 8 FINANCIAL BREAKTHROUGHS

- By setting concrete goals and timelines, you can protect yourself from procrastination, which can derail you.
- Protect yourself from the impact of taxes by using tax-advantaged IRA and 401K retirement accounts, tax-loss harvesting, and Roth IRA conversions.
- Protect yourself from market downturns with secure investments and a diverse portfolio and manage your tolerance for risk.
- Protect yourself against identity theft with strong passwords and regular financial monitoring.
- Protect yourself against incorrect information by relying only on trusted resources for financial wisdom.

Cash Flow Today (3)

Manage your cash flow successfully with a solid cash flow enhancement plan that includes:

- Budget and review automatic drafts.
- Cash flow enhancement plan.
- Cash flow ideas and opportunities.
- Making money with your passion

Debt-to-Income Ratio (4)

- Address your debt-to-income ratio by managing your debt and liabilities.
- Recognize good and bad debt.
- Create your cash flow awareness.
- Build and increase your credit score.

Liquidity (5)

Improving your liquidity cannot be overrated. Make sure that every pile of money you make has a purpose.

Some of the most essential purposes include:

- Preparing a 6-month emergency fund.
- Preparing a 12-month fund for business opportunities and growth.
- Acquiring access to capital and funding and educating yourself about the role banks play and relationship capital.

THE 8 FINANCIAL BREAKTHROUGHS

Future Income and Net Worth (6)

Focus on building your future income and net worth by developing the financial conversations you need to succeed.

- Develop your future lifestyle and retirement plan.
- Prepare for wealth accumulation and distribution when you move beyond your working years.
- Build your net worth to benefit yourself, your family, and your future.

Legacy and Succession Plan (7)

- Create the legacy and succession plan you and your family deserve.
- Establish a life insurance trust.
- Create your will and trust to build your succession and family legacy plan.
- Build your legacy every day.
- Find a good estate attorney.
- Find a good CPA.

Accountability (8)

Accountability leads you to achieve each of these financial breakthroughs.

To stay accountable, you need to:

- Select a responsibility and accountability coach.
- Appoint a financial professional.
- Set up your family office—the team you build will help you create present and future wealth.
- Be a legacy creator to achieve financial freedom.

Build a Winning Team

My heroes are sports greats like Kobe Bryant, Michael Jordan, and Muhammad Ali. I played football and basketball as a kid, and my work ethic affected that. I was willing to be coached to achieve higher levels, and I love the idea of being a coach. I might have gone in that direction if coaching kids' sports teams paid well.

Sports teach many things, like leadership, teamwork, and perseverance. They also teach the importance of being competitive and playing to win.

My reason for being is to help, coach, lead, and support others in becoming the legends in their families and

THE 8 FINANCIAL BREAKTHROUGHS

changing their family trees for the better forever. In short, I want to be the best legacy coach ever. I want to help 1,000 people make over $1,000,000 in income for life and give the next generation a tenfold head start.

Those important beliefs drive my work and help me build wealth. I want to help others enhance their lifestyles, who they are, and who they can become, just as I did. It is all based on leadership and team building.

I believe you need a team to win at anything.

My focus is to promote team building and leadership to everyone who is coachable and willing to give their best each day to become a legend.

Becoming a legend starts with finding the right financial choices, educating yourself about them, and utilizing them for your benefit. Once you do, you can be responsible for attaining the abundant life you deserve.
Committing is the key to winning in life.

Having a talented team and a clear vision and plan to attain your eight financial breakthroughs is the way to success in business and life.

As the Roman poet Virgil once said,

FPN INNOVATION TEAM

"Fortune sides with him who dares."

Once I shaped my vision, I was able to help others shape theirs, too, through my company, FPN–Financial Pro Network. I can help you realize these breakthroughs and ensure your vision, too.

"If you make meaning, you'll make money."

Guy Kawasaki

THE 8 FINANCIAL BREAKTHROUGHS

The initial step in "The 8 Financial Breakthroughs" is achieving Financial Awareness. By completing this book, you have already set yourself on the correct path.

Allow us to guide you through the remaining breakthroughs. This process begins with a discovery call, during which we dedicate 15 minutes to assess your current financial standing and, more crucially, define your future financial goals.

Following this, our expert financial professionals will diligently analyze your situation. We will explore the financial marketplace to identify the best products and services tailored to your needs, formulating a strategic plan to achieve your future objectives.

Do not procrastinate. Start building a financial foundation today.

We believe the information in this book is the ultimate guide to building Wealth for your financial Future. Let's connect soon.

FPN INNOVATION TEAM

Write Down Your Important Goals

"The Pain of Remaining the Same is Greater than the
Pain of Change"
Alvin Darien II

THE 8 FINANCIAL BREAKTHROUGHS

Made in the USA
Columbia, SC
22 July 2025